Stepping Up

Stepping Up

THE STORY OF
Curt Flood

AND HIS FIGHT FOR BASEBALL PLAYERS' RIGHTS

by Alex Belth

A Karen & Michael Braziller Book

PERSEA BOOKS / NEW YORK

Requests for permission to reprint or make photocopies and for any other information should be addressed to the publisher:

Persea Books, Inc.
853 Broadway
New York, NY 10003

Library of Congress Cataloging-in-Publication Data

Belth, Alex.
    Stepping up : the story of Curt Flood and his fight for baseball players' rights / Alex Belth.
        p. cm.
    ISBN 0-89255-321-9 (hardcover : alk. paper)
    1. Flood, Curt, 1938- 2. Baseball players—United States—
Biography. 3. African American baseball players—Biography. I. Title.
    GV865.F45B45 2006
    796.357092—dc22

                                2005028142

Design by Rita Lascaro
First Edition
Printed in the United States of America

For my grandfather, Nathan Belth, who showed me that good writing is the result of discipline and determination, and my great friend Marylou Leddon, who made me believe that I could accomplish anything I wanted so long as I was committed to putting in the work.

Contents

LIST OF PHOTOGRAPHS AND CHARTS

Foreword

When Curt Flood and I were traded from the St. Louis Cardinals to the Philadelphia Phillies in a seven-player exchange at the end of the 1969 season, I can't say that I was happy about the news. I had played my entire major league career for St. Louis and had gone to the World Series three times with that team. But at the time, there really wasn't anything players could do to influence for whom they played. The Players Association, which is now the most powerful union in all of sports, was still in its infancy, its resolve yet to be tested. I was sad to leave the Cardinals but prepared myself to join the Phillies.

However, Curt decided that he wasn't going to go along with the trade. He felt that after twelve years in the game, he had earned the right to offer his services to the highest bidder. He decided not to report to the Phillies and to take Major League Baseball to court to legally challenge its reserve system, which gave a player no right to determine where he played. The news shocked the baseball establishment. Initially, it shocked me. I said to Curt, "Do you really want to do this? Do you know what you are doing?"

Curt considered the matter seriously. He spoke with Marvin

Miller, the head of the Players Association, and thought long and hard about what he was about to do. And when he eventually addressed the union representatives from each team and received financial backing from the union to proceed with his suit, the least surprised person was me. The one thing that I remember most about Curt was that his preparation was nonpareil. In retrospect, I realize that if anybody in baseball was going to challenge the reserve clause it was Curt, because he was so meticulous in his preparation for any endeavor, be it athletic or otherwise.

An enormously gifted ballplayer, Curt was the quintessential professional who worked exceedingly hard at his craft. He played hurt. In fact, you couldn't get him out of the lineup. We wouldn't have won two World Series without him. A fine offensive player, he could also chase a fly ball down with the best, including Willie Mays. He used every advantage that he could, quizzing the pitchers on where they would pitch certain batters in specific counts so he would know where the ball would likely be hit. I can remember squatting behind the plate and seeing the blur of Curt moving around the outfield as a pitch was delivered based on who was hitting and on what type of pitch Curt knew I must have called for.

And Curt was a fearless hitter. Don Drysdale, the fireballing Hall of Famer from the Dodgers, called Flood the toughest out in the National League. Now, if you only knew how tough Don Drysdale was to hit against if you were right-handed. He knocked everybody down. But Curt was never rattled. He always stood his ground. He didn't strike out a lot and wasn't intimidated. As a batter, if he had a flaw it was that he gave himself up too much: he sacrificed himself too much for the good of the team. For instance, if there was a man on second base, Curt would always try to advance him to third base. A guy like Curt, who hit over .300 regularly, could have tried to pad his statistics by swinging for the fences. But he was a team player. He must have given himself up something like thirty times a year. If he had been more selfish, he could have had five more hits a year and raised his average maybe ten points, a big deal since in those days we all had one-year contracts; your batting average often determined whether you got a raise.

So he was the consummate team player. Johnny Edwards, who played with the Cards for one year, pointed that out to me when he came over in 1968. He said, "You know, I've never played with anybody else who went oh-for-four and still *genuinely* rooted for his teammates to get hits." But Curt was invested in the success of everyone, not merely in personal achievement or gain.

Therefore, it was a cruel irony that when Curt went ahead with his lawsuit, the baseball establishment portrayed him as an angry, selfish individual. Nothing could have been further from the truth. For his principled stand, he gave up a salary of $100,000—a considerable sum in those days—as well as any future in baseball management or coaching. He cared sincerely about the well-being of his fellow players, as well as the game of baseball itself. His sacrifice helped raise the general consciousness about the inequities in the game's financial structure. Not long after Curt's struggle ended, the players won the right to free agency—the right to determine for themselves for whom they worked. It took a man of Curt's strength and moral conviction to initiate this change.

Curt sacrificed his livelihood to ensure that in the future, the men who ran the game would not treat players like chattel, and today, ballplayers are multimillionaires. All of them owe a debt of gratitude to Curt and what he did. Thanks to Alex Belth's *Stepping Up*, you can now read about this remarkable man for yourself.

—Tim McCarver

Stepping Up

Prologue
October 8, 1969

Curt Flood was in bed when the call came, and bed was exactly where he wanted to be. For the first time in three years, his team, the St. Louis Cardinals, was not in the playoffs. It had been a long, difficult season, and now that it was over, he cherished the rest. Outside, the leaves were changing colors, and Flood was planning a change of scenery. He was leaving for Europe to spend part of the off-season recuperating.

The call came early—too early. A call so early in the morning from the front office could mean only one thing. On the other end of the line was Jim Toomey, assistant to general manager Bing Devine. Toomey said that he had some bad news. Flood had been traded to the Philadelphia Phillies.

Still groggy with sleep, Flood was speechless. He was thirty-one years old and his success had been hard-earned. He had grown up poor—a kid in the ghetto, hungry for attention. He had survived the indignities of the racist South during his time in the minor leagues in the 1950s. He had persevered through the accumulated injuries sustained over a fourteen-year professional career in an era when a black player couldn't afford to take a day off.

But in spite of the obstacles and the personal toll they took on him, Flood had prospered. In twelve years with the Cardinals, he'd won seven Gold Glove awards and been an All-Star three times. The team had won the league championship three times with him as its center fielder; it had won the World Series twice.

Flood was well aware of the dubious loyalties of baseball's upper management: he had already been traded once in his career, and players were traded unceremoniously all the time. Still, St. Louis was one of the classiest organizations in the game, and Flood had always been duly rewarded for his efforts. In turn, he'd adopted St. Louis as his home. He had business interests there, and a life that he'd spent over a decade creating. Now he was bound for Philadelphia, a city some considered one of the most racist in the league, and there was nothing he could do about it—nothing he could have done to prevent it.

In the fall of 1969, many aspects of American life were in the throes of change. While baseball was often seen as a kind of refuge from these troubles, the sport was not exempt from the spirit of revolution that permeated the country. The game's power structure was shifting. For generations players had accepted their playing conditions as immutable and the owners' word as final. They had done as they were told. Now, slowly, they were beginning to wonder why they shouldn't have at least some control over their professional lives.

Flood was from Oakland, home of the Black Panthers, and neighbor to the University of California at Berkeley, an epicenter of political activity. He was more politically conscious than most ballplayers and admired other athletes who had stood up for what they believed in—boxer Muhammad Ali and Olympic track stars Tommie Smith and John Carlos. For Flood, his own powerlessness in the face of his employers' whims was one such injustice. That baseball players had no control over where or for whom they played seemed totally un-American to him.

Flood could keep his mouth shut, accept the trade, and continue to make a handsome living, or he could risk everything he had—his livelihood, his reputation, and his future. Deep down, he sensed that this was his moment to take a stand. He didn't know it then, sitting alone in his nineteenth floor apartment, but what he did next would help change forever the sport he'd played and loved since he was a boy.

Chapter One
The Fastest Kid on the Block
(1938–1955)

Charles Curtis Flood was born in Houston, Texas, on January 18, 1938. His mother Laura had boarded a Pullman train days earlier to make the trip to her mother's home in Quincy, Louisiana, to give birth—a common practice among African Americans at the time. An intrepid woman in her mid-thirties, Laura traveled alone and without much money. She was already mother to five children, all of whom she'd left at home in Oakland, California, with her husband, Herman. The trip was a week long, but Laura, eight months pregnant, was determined to do it.

Laura never made it to Quincy. Curt came early, and the two of them settled in Texas for about a year before returning to Oakland. Whether Laura decided to stay in Houston because she didn't have the money to return or because she didn't feel well enough to travel with a newborn is unclear. In any case, Curt had her to himself for the first year of his life.

Laura and Herman had moved from the Deep South to West Oakland, a poor, dilapidated neighborhood, several years earlier. World War II had brought an influx of jobs, making Oakland an attractive destination for the Floods and many other southern black families, for whom work was scarce. However, those who came to the city in search of work and a better life were often bitterly disappointed. Racism on the West Coast was nearly as pervasive as in the South, if not as overt. Though racial segregation was not legal, de facto segregation restricted the areas in which black families could live and severely limited their job opportunities.

Though she came from a studious family, Laura worked as a house cleaner and seamstress. She always had more than one job, as the Floods needed to work as much as they could, in whatever way they could, to provide basic support for their children. When she wasn't at work, Laura earned money at home by mending clothes and, during World War II, parachutes. Herman, meanwhile, was a custodian at a hospital, where he normally logged nothing short of a seventy-two-hour workweek. The Floods believed in the American Dream: they thought that if they worked hard enough, good things would happen for them. Yet, like many other poor couples, they paid a severe price for their labor. Laura was often beleaguered and weary when she was home with the children, drained from the mental and physical demands put on her. Herman barely saw his kids at all, and when he did it was usually in carrying out his duties as house enforcer: if one of them got into trouble with Laura, she would send the child to Herman, who would whip him or her with a belt. Curt saw his father cry on more than one occasion because he often spent more time disciplining his children than playing with them. And both parents drank to help cope with the stresses of their lives.

While times were hard, Laura and Herman did provide for their children: There was always food on the table in the Flood home, though there were rarely second helpings to be had. Still, the kids wore hand-me-down clothes and had no privacy. (The four Flood children who still lived at home—Curt, Herman Jr., Barbara, and Carl—all shared a room and slept on army surplus bunk beds.) In an era when most families' main source of entertainment was a radio in the living room, it's not a given that the Floods had even that. Instead, they made their own music. Laura played the piano, and Herman played several instruments, including the guitar. Neither had any technical training—they were completely self-taught. Together, they would play for their children when they had the time and energy, but given their demanding schedules, the children received only sporadic attention.

Curt's older brother Carl found the surest way of getting noticed that any kid knows: he got in trouble. Often. He was hanging out with hustlers and hoodlums by the time he was thirteen. He started stealing. For fun, he would build small bombs out of metal scraps and set them off with his friends. Though he was bright and talented, Carl was seduced by street life. As a result, he required most of what limited parental attention existed in the Flood house.

As the youngest child, Curt had to fight to grab his parents' interest. After spending the first year of his life with just his mother, he now had to scramble to be considered. In the pecking order of the Flood family, Curt came last, and there was little he could do about it.

Curt learned a tough lesson early on: life was not fair. He saw his parents work themselves to the bone and receive the bare minimum in return. They were well meaning, but exhaustion and alcohol distanced them from their children. Watching his parents also taught him that determination and discipline were going to be essential if he wanted to achieve anything. Having talent or charm would not be enough (as Carl would learn). Hard work was required for advancement, though it didn't guarantee anything.

One thing that helped to keep the Flood kids out of harm's way was an interest in art. All of the children showed some talent for drawing and painting; Curt and Carl possessed the makings of real artists. Herman provided them with what art supplies he could afford. There were few scenes as comforting for the Flood parents as the sight of their children sprawled out on the living room floor, engrossed in their drawings. The kids were able to pass the time using their imagination, momentarily safe from life on the streets.

But art wasn't Curt's only talent. Toward the end of World War II, when he was five or six years old, Flood discovered that he was the fastest kid on his block. Though he was a runt, small and skinny, he was especially coordinated for a youngster and could throw and hit a baseball better than any kid his age in the neighborhood. In fact, Carl was the only kid of any age who was a superior player.

At this time, baseball was the most popular game in the country, truly the National Pastime. It was played everywhere—in the cities, in the burgeoning suburbs, and in the countryside—by people of all ages and backgrounds. There was organized ball for kids, as well as semi-pro ball and numerous industrial leagues, where factory workers competed against each other. The minor leagues, independently run operations that offered quality baseball, were popular as well.

And of course, there was Major League Baseball. The big leagues, though, were still entirely segregated, so the best black ballplayers played in their own leagues, the Negro Leagues, which began around World War I. These boasted their own legendary stars like Rube Foster, Oscar Charleston, Satchel Paige, and Josh Gibson, who were just as famous to black fans as Joe DiMaggio and Bob Feller were to whites.

Nationally, horse racing and boxing joined baseball as the most popular American sports. Boxing, in particular, took on a particular significance for African Americans when Joe Louis became heavyweight champion in 1939. Every time Louis fought, it was an event in black communities across the country. Everything would stop, and people would gather around a radio to listen to the fight. Louis was considered a god, but baseball was the foremost sport of the era. Other team sports like football and basketball, popular on the high school and college level, were still thought of more as recreation than serious professions.

By the time Flood was seven or eight, he was playing with the older kids; soon after, he could outrun and outhit most of them. Curt was used to being the smallest and the youngest at home, so playing against older and bigger kids did not intimidate him. If anything, having big brothers to teach him the ropes probably helped him when it came to playing against other kids.

Curt idolized his brother Carl in particular, who was in turn protective of him, making sure not to involve his kid brother in any unlawful behavior. It was an unspoken pact the two would share throughout their adolescence: Curt did not ask about Carl's activities, and Carl did not invite him along. In spite of this, when Curt was nine or ten, he did have one brush with the law. One afternoon, he was walking the streets, as he sometimes did during idle time. He meandered up to a sawdust factory and saw an empty delivery truck, just like one Carl had recently swiped. Curt climbed into driver's seat, held the steering wheel, and pretended to steer. Then he noticed that the key was in the ignition. He turned it over and somehow reached his foot all the way down to the clutch. The truck lurched forward. It rolled along, and Flood, as if in a dream, maneuvered the wheel. After a few blocks, he lost control. The truck crashed into a parked car. Jolted, Flood was dazed after the impact. When he gathered himself, he must have felt relieved to be unharmed. But that relief was likely replaced by a sense of dread.

Shortly thereafter, the police picked him up. Curt's mind raced. How much trouble was he in? How badly would his father beat him? About an hour after the crash, the police dropped Curt off at the detention center. By that time, he was quivering. He was escorted to a cell and locked inside. Alone.

Curt stayed in the cold, hard cell waiting for his parents to get him, but they didn't come. He remained there overnight. In the morning, he stood up and looked through the small glass window. He was exhausted, frightened, and hungry. Then he saw his brother Carl walk past his cell, looking glum. He had been picked up for joyriding in a truck, too, and didn't know that his younger brother was a prisoner as well. It was a distressing day for the Flood parents—the first time that they had to come to the detention center to get not one but two of their sons. Herman informed Curt that his little caper had caused $300 worth of damage, which would take weeks, if not months, to pay off. Herman was furious, shaking with anger, and he beat his youngest child without mercy.

In the end, the truck incident was a gift to Curt: it scared him straight. The same could not be said for Carl. The beatings he received when he misbehaved only strengthened his defiance. He was incredibly bright but incurably rebellious. He would repeatedly tempt fate, always getting burned and suffering in the end. Through the years, Curt could only watch, helpless to change the direction of his brother's life.

The Floods lived close to Bushrod Park, one of the most famous playgrounds in Oakland. It was there, in 1947, that Curt became the catcher for Junior's Sweet Shop, his first experience in organized baseball. Curt was probably too small to be a catcher, but Carl was a pitcher on the squad, and Curt wanted to be his receiver. Laura did not know that her baby was playing the roughest position on the field, and her sons weren't about to tell her. The team was in the police-sponsored midget league for kids aged nine through eleven. It played all around Oakland, chauffeured around town in a police wagon, the players likely never giving a second thought to who might have been handcuffed in the back of the wagon the night before.

The unofficial mayor of Bushrod Park—coaching the kids, organizing the leagues, and offering instruction—was George Powles, a squat, middle-aged white man with a buzz cut. While he looked like someone black kids in the 1940s might have kept their distance from—a gruff, white authority figure—Powles was anything but a racist. A natural with children, he cared for the kids who showed up to play ball at the park, regardless of the color of their skin.

Powles had tried unsuccessfully to play professionally when he was young but found his calling years later at McClymonds High, a small, predominantly black school in West Oakland, where he coached baseball and basketball. In summers, he coached baseball teams at all different levels, from Little League on up through Legion Ball, which was for teens aged fifteen and up. In 1949, his Legion Ball team would win the national title; in 1950, for the first time in the thirty-two-year history of the league, which boasted 16,500 teams nationally, his squad repeated as champions. Incredibly, fourteen of the team's twenty-five players during those two years would end up playing professionally.

In the 1940s and 1950s, Powles served as mentor and father figure to some of the greatest athletes to come out of Oakland. Among them was Bill Russell, who had been cut from his junior varsity basketball team but who flourished as a varsity player under Powles, later powering the Boston Celtics to a remarkable eleven titles in his thirteen years with the team; the speedy Vada Pinson, who would eventually collect over 2,700 hits in the majors; and Frank Robinson, a shy boy but a fierce competitor who would go on to a Hall of Fame career in the big leagues and in 1975 become the first black man to manage a major league team when he became the skipper of the Cleveland Indians. In total, well over a hundred kids Powles coached had professional careers in sports.

Like all of the best youth-league coaches, George Powles was as interested in preparing his boys for life—showing them the discipline and hard work it would take to be a success—as he was in trying to win ballgames. Powles instilled confidence and focus in them, influencing many of his boys, not just the ones who went on to be professional athletes. He wanted them to think for themselves. On the field, they were schooled to be aggressive but intelligent: to take the extra base when the ball was hit to an outfielder with a weak throwing arm and to decoy base runners into thinking a ball had been caught when it hadn't.

Away from the park, Powles opened up his home to his boys. It was common for a gang of them—ten, twenty, thirty strong—to hang out at his comfortable if modest home. Powles's wife welcomed the kids—black and white—with open arms. They raided her kitchen, and she fed them cookies and ice cream. Some would start up a card game in the kitchen, while others gathered around Powles as he told stories or offered coaching tips. The boys Powles coached revered him and often spoke of him years later as one of the defining figures of their lives. (According to Russell, the faith Powles showed by putting him on the varsity team was monumental. "By that one gesture," Russell later wrote in his autobiography, *Go Up for Glory*, "I believe that man saved me from becoming a juvenile delinquent. If I hadn't had basketball, all of my energies and frustrations would surely have been carried in some other direction.")

Curt made an immediate impression on Powles, even at the age of nine. It isn't difficult to imagine why. He was curious, articulate, and eager to please. What more could a teacher ask for? Powles had a lot of kids who were dedicated to him, but Curt had a self-confidence off the field that many of the other boys didn't possess. He was around Powles constantly. During basketball season, he would wait for the coach's practices with the older boys to finish; then Powles would hit ground balls to him in the school gymnasium.

Baseball gave Curt a true sense of purpose, of identity. When he played, he mattered. When he wasn't competing or practicing for his own team, he would travel with the older kids on the American Legion squad, warming up the pitchers or catching batting practice. In between innings, the skinny kid would sprint around the outfield and wow the spectators with his speed and timing. He had an instinct for tracking down fly balls and would make trick catches to entertain those looking on. He was a marvel on the baseball field.

If 1947 was a significant year for baseball in the life of Curt Flood, it was even more significant for professional baseball, as Jackie Robinson broke the sport's color barrier, becoming the first black man in the twentieth century to play in the major leagues. (Two black brothers, Moses Fleetwood Walker and Welday Walker both played briefly in the majors in the 1880s.)

There were no specific laws that had barred blacks from the majors, but an unspoken "gentleman's agreement" among the owners prevented them from playing. This all changed when Branch Rickey, president of the Brooklyn Dodgers, decided to bring an African American to the National

League. Rickey had built an extraordinary career in baseball. He had established the St. Louis Cardinals as a first class organization in the 1920s and 1930s by creating a "farm system," acquiring minor league clubs and using them as a training ground to develop players for his major league team. It was a huge success: St. Louis captured National League pennants in 1926, 1928, 1930, 1931, and 1934, winning the World Series in three of those seasons. After the Cardinals won the World Series again in 1942, Rickey left St. Louis and became the general manager, president, and part-owner of the Brooklyn Dodgers. Several years later, his next innovation was to integrate baseball.

While Rickey was no racist, his impulse to integrate was not solely humanitarian. First and foremost, he was a capitalist. By hiring blacks at bargain prices, he gave his team a competitive edge over the rest of the National League. The opportunity to choose from among all of the talented black ballplayers in country was too good to pass up. Not only that, Rickey would be able to use his clout to get what he wanted on his terms, at his price.

Jackie Robinson was not selected by Rickey because he was necessarily the greatest black baseball player; many Negro Leaguers believed there were others among their ranks who were superior. But Robinson showed the kind of character necessary to withstand the abuse and torment he was bound to encounter from a largely hostile public. He was college educated and had served in the military. Though proud, he was savvy enough to put any anger aside for the larger cause. Well before the start of the civil rights movement, he understood that what he was doing could have a terrific impact on blacks across the country.

The importance of Robinson in African American communities cannot be overstated. He was national news, a tremendous point of pride. Newspapers and radio stations kept black Americans informed of his every move, and people talked about him wherever they gathered—in taverns, schools, and barber shops. Every game he performed well in was a cause for celebration. And while Robinson faced more than his fair share of discrimination from fans and opposing teams alike along the way, he was a box office draw. "Jackie's nimble, Jackie's quick, Jackie's making the turnstiles click," Wendell Smith wrote in the *Pittsburgh Courier* on May 31, 1947.

Still, Robinson's story must have seemed a distant adventure to Flood and his contemporaries. The major leagues did not play in California in 1947. Instead, the Pacific Coast League (PCL) *was* the big leagues if you lived on the West Coast. The PCL was a successful, high-level minor league that featured the best baseball west of St. Louis (the westernmost major league town), with teams in Los Angeles, Hollywood, San Francisco, Oakland, San Diego, Sacramento, Seattle, and Portland. The level of play wasn't quite major league caliber, but it was excellent nonetheless. Unlike teams in other minor leagues, those in the PCL were generally not major league-affiliated: they played to win, not to produce talent for a parent club.

Perhaps more than Robinson, a PCL player like Artie Wilson was someone whom Flood and his peers admired. A whiz of a shortstop, Wilson became the first black man to play for the hometown Oakland Oaks when he was traded there in 1949. (The PCL had been integrated a year earlier.) Wilson led the league in average and stolen bases in 1949, and he was a hero for the local kids. He remained a league standout into the mid-1950s, and probably would have been a useful major league player. But he was not star material and only had a brief stint in the big leagues.

What Wilson and Robinson offered boys like Flood was something that was a birthright for white kids: the dream of playing professional ball. They also gave them the opportunity to view themselves differently. Robinson offered a black kid the chance to look at sports and say, *Here's a playing field where I can be viewed as equals with a white kid, where I can be judged on my own merits, pure and simple.*

Flood didn't necessarily think of going to watch people play baseball when he could be having fun playing baseball himself, but one day when he was about thirteen he did get to see the pros play. With a group of friends, Flood went to Oaks Park in Emeryville to catch the Oaks and Artie Wilson in action. When he arrived at the ballpark, he was spellbound: It was the most beautiful baseball field he had ever seen. The game was underway, and there was a full house, five thousand people—not many by major league standards, but probably the most Curt had ever seen gathered in one place. The smell of peanuts, beer, and smoke were in the air, and an organist played between innings. For a kid used to the concrete streets of the slums, it must have seemed like a slice of heaven.

Contrary to what one might expect, Flood's experience with white people during his youth—an experience that would later help shape his outlook on life—was generally positive. This started, of course, with Powles, and was furthered by his relationships with Jim Chambers and Sam Bercovich.

Chambers was the art teacher at Herbert Hoover Junior High School, a free spirit who bristled at the traditional conventions of the classroom. He was drawn to Flood because of his obvious skills as an artist—skills that the boy had never really taken seriously. Chambers provided him with a sense of art history, taught him how to look at paintings and sculptures from an artist's perspective. Flood had the gift of drawing and

The young Flood poses for his American Legion team in 1956. Though small in stature, his powerful wrists and forearms gave him surprising power as a hitter. (Source: The Oakland Museum)

painting subjects with a high degree of likeness. He excelled at portraiture. Chambers encouraged him to find the telling detail in each subject he painted that would convey something specific about the subject's personality. In the three years they spent together, he pushed Flood to be expressive, to develop his own style. Flood responded and grew from a kid with some talent into a budding artist.

By the time Flood started high school at McClymonds, he had gotten an afternoon job working at Bercovich's Furniture, which was run by Sam Bercovich, a Jewish businessman whose father had opened the store during World War I. Bercovich was a keen sports fan who would grow to be something of a legend in the Oakland sports community as a dear friend of Al Davis, owner of the Oakland Raiders. For years, if you played professional ball in Oakland—whether for the Raiders, the Oaks, or, later, the A's—you bought your furniture at Bercovich's.

Bercovich's had been sponsoring youth baseball teams since 1929. George Powles coached all of these teams, so Bercovich had known Flood for some time. Initially, Flood did various odd jobs around the store. He dusted the shelves and swept the floors. He helped unload deliveries. But in time he took on more interesting work, helping to design the window displays. He was the ideal worker: always on his toes, enterprising and alert. He also had natural charisma. One day, Flood made a delivery to a local woman. Several hours later, the woman came into the store and told Bercovich that she had been so taken with Flood that she was going to buy a new dining room set on the spot. Bercovich was impressed. "He was born to be bright," he said of Flood years later.

Around this time, Flood moved out of his parents' home to live with his sister Barbara, who had gotten married and had a child. Barbara worked during the day and needed a baby-sitter during the evenings, as she'd recently separated from her husband, John Henry Johnson. Johnson, a running back for the San Francisco 49ers, was part of the team's "Million Dollar Backfield" with quarterback Y. A. Title and halfbacks Hugh McElhenny and Joe Perry. Though Flood had been never particularly close with his brother-in-law, he had, through him, glimpsed what it was like to be a professional athlete: the focus it required, the time away from home, the constant injuries.

Flood was developing into an outstanding young baseball player. The kid who used to dazzle Legion crowds at the age of nine with his fielding prowess continued to impress. He was short but strong. When Flood was fourteen, he competed favorably with seventeen- and eighteen-year-olds. The following year, Flood hit three balls over the four hundred foot fence in left field at Bushrod Park, an achievement that wasn't soon forgotten in West Oakland. In his second year at McClymonds, Flood played with Frank Robinson, who was a senior. Robinson played the game with a relentless passion: no one wanted to get in his way. Robinson led the team in home runs that year, but Flood led in hitting with a .400 batting average.

It actually wasn't until Flood's last year of Legion ball that he moved to center field. After having started as a catcher, he then moved to shortstop; now he was switching to another crucial position. The spaciousness of the outfield appealed to him. There he could put his speed to good use. He loved the challenge of swallowing up long drives that were hit in the gap, or soft fly balls that looked like they were going to dunk behind second base for a hit.

Flood had always been a hard working infielder, but until he moved to center field, he'd been known more for his hitting than for his fielding. He was something of an oddity: a small guy with pop in his bat. Like Hank Aaron or, decades later, Alfonso Soriano, he had strong wrists and forearms. He consistently led Powles's Legion team in hitting despite being only five and a half feet tall. In 1955, against a club from Utah, Flood slugged two home runs over the fence in Lodi, California. He also had a single with the bases loaded, and he ended the day with nine runs batted in. Flood powered the team to the California Legion title that season. In twenty-seven Legion games, he hit a staggering .620 with twelve doubles, five triples, and nine home runs.

During Flood's last two years of high school, it became increasingly apparent that he might have enough talent to play in the Pacific Coast League. Perhaps he would even play for the Oaks. At the time, the major leagues may still have seemed a pipe dream, though less so since the Cincinnati Reds inked Frank Robinson to a contract in 1953—for a miniscule amount, of course, compared to what coveted white prospects were given. Still, the fact that he signed at all perhaps gave Flood reason to hope.

Throughout high school, Flood continued to develop his skill as an artist, but the prospect of an entry-level job in advertising or as a draftsman paled in comparison to the idea of being a professional baseball player. Flood grew up watching his parents struggle to get by. He knew what was waiting for him if he stayed in Oakland. Though he had never courted trouble, the temptations of the street life would always be there, ready to sap the ambition out of him.

Professional scouts were constantly hanging around Powles's teams because of the wealth of talent they boasted. Several of Powles's scouting friends spoke with Flood and were struck by his demeanor: self-assured and cool but hungry and willing to learn. Flood was what scouts called "wound tight,"

Flood and Sam Bercovich pose together with a championship trophy in 1956. Bercovich gave Flood a job and deeply admired the young man. Their friendship would last for more than 40 years. (Source: The *Oakland Tribune* Collection, the Oakland Museum of California.)

which meant that while he was calm and confident on the outside, he was driven and competitive on the inside. But while his play had been strong—in 1955, he finished second in the Alameda Winter League in hitting at .412—there were serious doubts about his size. These doubts weren't unwarranted. Flood wasn't a middle-infielder, where you could survive as a smaller guy. He was playing center field, the glamor position of the era, where a player needed stamina and durability. Willie Mays and Mickey Mantle were center fielders. They were big, strapping athletes who possessed both incredible speed and power. Maybe Flood wouldn't be able to hold up physically. While scouts were intrigued by his determination and poise, they were far more excited about Vada Pinson, who was bigger, stronger, and faster.

Powles's main contact among scouts was Bobby Mattick, the Cincinnati Reds' West Coast man who had signed Frank Robinson and would later sign Pinson, too. Mattick could see that Flood had something more than raw physical talent. He was a fearless competitor, with resolve and intelligence that made him worth taking a chance on. Plus, he'd come cheap. In the fall of 1955, Mattick offered Flood a one-year contract for $4,000. Flood wasn't too small after all; he was going to be a professional ballplayer.

Although it had been years since Jackie Robinson had broken the color barrier, it was still an arduous journey for a black man to make it to the major leagues. In 1950, only 3 percent of major leaguers were black. In the following years Willie Mays, Ernie Banks, Hank Aaron, Roberto Clemente, and Frank Robinson would all emerge as legitimate stars, but these men were exceptional players: all five would one day be in the Hall of Fame. Many more players floundered in the minor leagues or weren't signed in the first place.

No matter how talented, black players didn't receive many breaks from the front offices. They weren't paid nearly as well as their white counterparts. Furthermore, not every team was committed to the idea of having African Americans on its roster. The New York Yankees, for instance, were the dominant, most wealthy team of the era, and these traits enabled the racism of their front office: they didn't recruit or promote black and Latin players to the big league club because they didn't need to in order to win. Instead, they spent more money on white players than any other major league team, which helped keep them rich in talent. It took New York until 1955 to field its first black player, the catcher Elston Howard. The Philadelphia Phillies didn't integrate until 1957, and the Detroit Tigers waited until 1958. The Boston Red Sox were the last team to integrate, waiting until 1959.

But most teams could not afford to ignore black baseball players if they wanted to stay competitive, and teams that aggressively recruited black players—for example, the Dodgers, the Giants, and the Indians—saw those investments pay immediate dividends. The bottom line was that the best black players were at least as good as the best white players, and those black players could be had for a fraction of what decent white prospects cost.

Flood had never left the Bay Area for any extended period of time. He was essentially a sheltered kid, and the Oakland ghetto in which he grew up was an insulated world: When *Brown vs. Board of Education* was upheld by the Supreme Court in 1954, desegregating public education, the news barely made a ripple through the city's black community. Now Flood would be reporting to spring training in Florida and then likely sent to play for a farm club somewhere in the South.

One afternoon, Powles took Flood aside. In no uncertain terms, he explained that his road to the majors was going to be harsh, not only because Flood was black, but because he was so small. Jackie Robinson and Minnie Minoso were big guys. Frank Robinson was a big guy. Flood was a shrimp, and therefore an easier target. And in order to make it to the major leagues, Flood would have to be better than—not merely as good as—his white counterparts. There were almost no jobs available for black or Latin utility infielders at the time; those spots were primarily the domain of white players. On the other hand, the better Flood performed, the more hostility he would face. He would have to learn how to handle bigotry and not let it stop him from excelling. Otherwise, he would find himself back home in Oakland before he knew it.

While Flood knew that Powles was right, he also thought he was up to the challenge. He had been considered a good kid, an achiever, by blacks and whites alike. Why shouldn't he feel confident? He didn't know the full extent of racism in professional ball or the segregated South, but he was about to find out all about it.

Chapter Two
"Have a Good Year and Get Out of Here": The Minors (1956–1957)

Violence against African Americans in the South intensified during the second half of the 1950s. In 1954, the *Brown vs. Board of Education* Supreme Court decision initiated an era of civil unrest. The following year, Emmet Till, a fourteen-year-old black kid from Chicago, was murdered in Mississippi, reportedly for whistling at a white woman. J. W. Milam, one of the men who killed Till, told *Look* magazine:

> As long as I live and can do anything about it, niggers are gonna stay in their place. Niggers ain't gonna vote where I live. If they did, they'd control the government. They ain't gonna go to school with my kids . . . "Chicago boy," I said [to Till], "I'm tired of 'em sending your kind down here to stir up trouble. Goddam you, I'm going to make an example of you—just so everybody can know how me and my folks stand."

Less than six months after Till was killed, Rosa Parks was arrested for refusing to give up her seat to a white man on a bus. Her arrest was a catalyst for the civil rights movement. Parks was dignified and intelligent, and her protest, involving something as essential as public transportation, was something that working-class blacks all over the country could identify with. On December 5, the Great Montgomery Bus Boycott began. It would last 381 days. Before it was three months old, Curt Flood arrived in the South to play professional baseball.

Like many of the black players of the period, Flood was visiting the South for the first time, and its ways came as a shock to the system. For their part, major league organizations did almost nothing to prepare their young black players for the kind of discrimination they might encounter in the minor leagues. Players were assigned with little regard for the risks they would encounter in certain leagues and cities.

Flood had received a brochure from the Reds months earlier, from which he learned that players stayed at ritzy-looking hotel called The Floridian during spring training. Already filled with expectations and excitement about playing ball professionally, he was, he would acknowledge in his autobiography, set soaring by the pictures of the hotel. The lobby was ornate, the rooms spacious and inviting. The major leagues were going to be first class all the way. Flood was also excited when he realized that Frank Robinson would be at the spring training camp, starting his fourth year in the Cincinnati organization. It would be like the old days at Bushrod Park back in Oakland.

However, nothing could have prepared him for the culture shock he was about to experience—not an old teammate, not all of George Powles's sage advice. Upon arriving in Florida, Flood went to get his luggage and noticed signs for the drinking fountains: one was marked White, the other Colored. Flood had never seen anything like this in Oakland, and for a moment he naïvely wondered if the signs distinguished club soda from Coca Cola.

Flood made his way to the hotel, where he hoped things would be better. Indeed, The Floridian was as fancy as he had imagined, and Flood was duly impressed. If this was how major leaguers lived, then everything was going to be okay. Flood strode to the front desk where a white clerk brusquely dismissed him. Confused, Flood informed him that he was with the Reds. Unmoved, the man dispatched a black porter to escort Flood away. The porter took Flood through a side door and hailed a taxi. Once he got Flood got into the back-seat, the porter told the black driver, "Ma Felder's."

Ma Felder's was a boardinghouse five miles out of town where black and Latin players stayed. Flood had assumed that he would be living in style as a professional prospect; instead he was given a blunt introduction to the Jim Crow South. Yes, he was a talented ballplayer who had an opportunity to make it to the big leagues one day—but in the South, he was a sec-ond-class citizen.

Upon arriving at Ma Felder's, Flood must have been relieved to see Frank Robinson among the players there, along with veteran ballplayers like Joe Black, Brooks Lawrence, George Crowe, and Bob Thurman. With the exception of Robinson, these men were well over ten years Flood's senior. Other than Lawrence, they had played in the Negro Leagues and had traveled a long, hard road to make the major leagues. In the Negro Leagues, players like Black and Crowe played up to three games a day, enduring terrible traveling conditions and lousy pay. If they were hurt, they were sent home, so they played through injuries.

Soon after Flood arrived at the big league camp, he was reassigned to the Reds' minor-league facility in Douglas, Georgia. The Reds noted Flood's ability as a centerfielder and liked that he could hit a little too. Yet he needed to hone his skills. The facility was a former military base, and the experience wasn't so different from army life: the food was terrible, and the four hundred players were housed in segregated barracks. From atop lookout towers, scouts and managers, the organization's talent evaluators, surveyed players on numerous fields in action all at once as they stretched in formation, performed sliding drills in a sand-pit, and played exhibition games all day long.

Each player was issued a small sign with a number, which he wore on his back. It was a cattle call, not an instructional league: players were there not to learn but to show whether they had the raw skills needed to play the game at a higher level. Issued 330 (a far cry from the single-digit number stars wore in the majors), Flood played hard and with purpose. He had a high baseball IQ from playing under Powles, which helped tremendously. He hit well, fielded well, and was unerring on the bases. His speed in the outfield was his greatest strength. The Reds sent him to the Class B High Point-Thomasville team in the Carolina League. That meant that Flood was skipping class C and D ball, a considerable accomplishment. The Reds clearly liked what they saw in him, though they didn't feel that he was ready to make the jump to the majors quite yet. After all, Frank Robinson, who was regarded as a better prospect, had spent three seasons in the minors. Flood took his assignment as a positive sign and figured that in no time at all he would join Robinson in Cincinnati. In honor of Jackie Robinson, Flood chose the number 42.

Today, through the technology of the Internet, where complete statistical data is available for virtually every player on every level of organized baseball, fans enjoy thorough and detailed access to the goings-on of the minor leagues, and some prospects are even celebrities before they even sign a contract. This was not the case in the 1950s. A diehard fan might be aware of a prospect playing in his region, but, otherwise, minor league players were virtually unknown.

The fifties were a devastating decade for the minors. In 1949, minor-league games drew almost 42 million spectators. A decade later, they attracted just 12 million. Major League Baseball was directly responsible for this decline. Its own attendance was down sharply, due in part to decay in the inner city neighborhoods that housed its parks, and it needed to broaden its fan base. Therefore, it went on the move. In 1953, the Boston Braves relocated to Milwaukee, where they would set attendance records and, in 1957, win a championship. The next year, the St. Louis Browns moved to Baltimore (a town with a rich minor league history), and in 1955, the A's moved from Philadelphia to Kansas City. Finally, when both the Giants and Dodgers moved from New York City to California in 1958, it signaled a new era for the game. Major League Baseball had raided minor league cities, and minor league teams didn't have the resources to compete for fans.

What's more, every major league team had by this point adopted Branch Rickey's farm system, so many of the remaining minor league clubs were big league owned. Their chief concern was not necessarily to win but to develop and nurture talent—which didn't necessarily make for great viewing. But perhaps the most critical factor in the demise of the minor leagues was the booming popularity of television. Both television and air conditioning became accessible to average Americans during the fifties; people didn't see the need to go out to the game when they could stay home and relax. If you lived in a hot, remote part of the country, why bother rooting for a rinky-dink minor league team when you could watch a major league team at home on television?

Flood's strong showing in his first spring training was even more significant when considering that competition for spots on a major league roster was even fiercer than it is today—especially for African Americans and Hispanics. At the time, there were only sixteen big league teams, not thirty, and many qualified utility players became lifelong minor leaguers because there wasn't room for them with the parent club. It was even tougher for a black player, who had little future as a backup and was often forced to play hurt for fear of being demoted or cut. Early in his minor league career, Frank Robinson was hit under the eye with a pitch and was hospitalized overnight. A couple of days later, he was back in the lineup.

In addition to enduring physical travails, black players endured constant verbal abuse from the fans. It was as much a part of their experience as learning how to hit a curve ball or getting knocked down with a brush-back pitch. The tension and volatility was palpable, as black players like Flood were showered with chants of "spook" and "nigger" on a regular basis, stomaching extreme hostility from people who should have been their supporters. Those players who endured and thrived had to possess not only talent but emotional fortitude as well.

Many young black players emulated the non-confrontational tact that Jackie Robinson adopted during his early years with the Dodgers. For those born in the South, like Ernie Banks, the great slugger for the Cubs, and Hank Aaron, who would become the all-time home run champion, the racist treatment they received didn't come as a surprise. (Still, the death threats Aaron received while playing in Montgomery, Alabama, can't have been easy to ignore.) Some players responded, though. Bill White, a slick fielding first baseman who would later play with Flood, was from Ohio. He did not suffer racist goons lightly. In 1953, White, then nineteen years old, was the only black player in the Carolina League. He yelled back at his hecklers. On one occasion, he gave the crowd the finger, and he and his teammates had to arm themselves with bats to protect themselves as they made their way to the team bus after the game.

One of Flood's first experiences playing in High Point-Thomasville involved a father and his four sons, all of whom had front row seats. The father instructed his boys to chant "black bastard" at Flood. For nine innings, he carefully monitored them to make sure they were doing it to his satisfaction. But worse than the abuse that Flood received from the fans was his neglect by virtually everyone on his team. Flood was used to getting support from his coaches. Now it was as if he didn't exist. And players, white and black, treated him with antipathy—at the very least, he was competition for them. Flood was effectively frozen out of the social fabric of the team, and during the first few weeks of the season, he would return to his room at night and break down in tears.

The Hi-Toms, as the team was called, played eight games a week: one a day from Monday through Saturday, and a double header on Sunday. When the team traveled, Flood was restricted from eating in restaurants with his teammates. He would remain in the stifling bus, hot and sweaty, still in his dirty uniform, unable to join them. Flood had to go the back door of the kitchen to be served his dinner. Sometimes he wouldn't even be allowed to do that, and a teammate would bring him food on the bus. When the bus stopped at a gas station, Flood was not permitted to use the rest room. If he had to relieve himself, he would have to do so along the highway, where he would try to hide himself from the traffic along the side of the bus.

The road trips bothered some black players more than the catcalls at the ballpark. White players got to stay in air-conditioned hotels, while blacks stayed at a local version of Ma Felder's—when they were lucky. At least that meant home-cooked meals. The alternative was a local YMCA, which often had no shower. Even getting to and from the park could be an ordeal. White cabbies often refused to pick up black players, and even black cabbies would sometimes charge them more than they would white customers.

For Flood, the alienation, anxiety, and humiliation he experienced cut him deeply, but after the first few weeks he became accustomed to the isolation and developed into a cool customer. He showed little emotion, positive or negative. He simply played at full tilt and kept to himself. Being cool for a black man in the fifties was a posture, a way of expressing his disgust and anger at what he had to put up with without becoming unhinged. Black athletes couldn't be brash or outspoken if they valued their lives.

At times, Flood grew so frustrated with his estranged teammates that he even entertained the notion of sabotaging games by "accidentally" dropping a fly ball, just to spite them. He had too much professional pride to actually go through with this plan, and in the second half of the season, relations with his teammates relaxed somewhat. Performance is a great equalizer, and Flood was whaling the ball and playing well in the field. Perhaps because of his performance, Flood became more comfortable sticking up for himself as the season went along. One day, a young black boy ran onto the field during batting practice, swiped a ball from the field, and then ran off into the crowd—a common occurrence. One of Flood's teammates shouted a racist remark at the kid. Without hesitation, Flood went up to the player and made it perfectly clear that he wasn't going to tolerate that kind of talk anymore. The teammate didn't exactly apologize, but he did back off. Flood also developed ways to cope with abusive fans. *They're ignorant; they don't know any better,* he'd think. He would imagine pitiable explanations for why these people felt the need to abuse him—anything to keep the painful truth from breaking his spirit. It was essential to find a way to cope. Frank Robinson, for example, used to chant a mantra to himself: "Have a good year and get out of here, Have a good year and get out of here."

While the Hi-Toms found themselves in a pennant race late in the season, Flood went into a deep slump and saw his batting average drop to its lowest point of the year. By that point, he was utterly enervated from the heat, the rigorous schedule, and the tension of being a black player in the South. He had lost considerable weight, and was down to 135 pounds. Somehow, though, he recovered and batted close to .500 over the final three weeks of the season, leading his team to a first-place finish. (His game-winning home run on August 22 against the Wilson Tobs was a highlight.) Though the Hi-Toms were swept by Fayetteville in the playoffs, they'd had a great year.

Flood had had a great year, too—so great, in fact, that he won the league's Player of the Year award for hitting .340 with 29 home runs and 128 runs scored. This caught the attention of the Reds, and in September, he was called up to the big league club. Flood's hard work had paid off: he was going to the majors.

The Reds had been a perennially lackluster team for over a decade, having finished no higher than third place in the National League in that time. In 1956, however, they were surprisingly good, led by power hitters Ted Kluszewski, Wally Post, and the rookie Frank Robinson. In fact, the Reds had five players with more than twenty home runs, and the team tied a major league record for homers hit in a season with 221. Robinson was sensational, batting .290 with 38 home runs and 122 runs scored. He was the clear choice for the National League Rookie of the Year award. Cincinnati also set a club record for attendance, drawing 1,125,928 fans. The team competed with the Milwaukee Braves and the Brooklyn Dodgers all season but finally fell apart in mid-September.

Flood arrived with the Reds just as the team was running out of steam, but it didn't matter much to him. While the Reds players and their fans were deflated by how the season was ending, it was a charged atmosphere for Flood. In the majors, the balls were whiter, the uniforms crisper, and the lights brighter. Tens of thousands of fans packed the stadiums. The teams traveled by plane, not some old bus with cigarette holes in the upholstery. Players didn't need to tend to their own uniforms before and after the game. They didn't pack or carry their bags either. Somebody did that for them. After the game, instead of peanut butter and jelly sandwiches and maybe some candy bars, there was a spread—cold cuts, cheese, fruit, juices, and pastries. And they didn't have to buy their own beer. It was already there, cold, waiting for them. When the Reds were in New York to play the Giants for a two-game series on September 11 and 12, Flood wrote letters on hotel stationary to his family, Powles, Bercovich, and Chambers, boasting about his big league life.

Flood's first major league appearance came in St. Louis on Sunday, September 9. In a 6-5 loss, Flood pinch-ran for catcher Smokey Burgess in the eighth inning and was left stranded on base. Three days later, at the Polo Grounds in New York, he struck out as a pinch hitter against Johnny Antonelli, the Giants ace, in his first major league at-bat. After that, he would have just a few uneventful appearances as a pinch runner before the end of the season, but whatever disappointment he felt about his quiet debut was overshadowed by his excitement at simply being a major leaguer.

As the season ended, Flood was called in to see the Reds general manager Gabe Paul to discuss next year's contract. The meeting was to be his first real encounter with baseball's reserve system—a lopsided, owner-friendly framework that eliminated any leverage a player, black or white, had when it came to negotiating his contract. The key to the reserve system lay in paragraph 10a of the players' standard contract. This clause, known as the option clause or reserve clause, stated that if a team and its player could not come to terms on a new contract, the club could simply renew the previous contract for an additional year without the player's consent. Since teams customarily signed players to one-year deals at the time, they could invoke the reserve clause indefinitely. What's more, by contract they could cut a player's salary up to 25 percent in the process. The players were powerless. Their only alternative was to retire.

Baseball's imbalanced system had an explanation: the sport was exempt from the antitrust laws that bound other industries. In 1922, a Supreme Court ruling, *Federal Baseball Club of Baltimore, Inc. v National League of Professional Baseball Clubs*, claimed that while baseball was a business, it was not interstate commerce and therefore was not subject to antitrust laws. In a decision that would become infamous, the acclaimed Justice Oliver Wendell Holmes wrote that baseball, driven by "personal effort, not related to production, is not a subject of commerce." The ruling was absurd. It allowed the owners to get away with murder. The players had no right of self-determination.

In his meeting with Paul, Flood reminded the general manager of how well he had performed. He thought his numbers spoke for themselves, and he expected a raise. As Flood recited each of his statistics, Paul frowned and shook his head. He told Flood that while the Reds were pleased with his progress, the organization was not in a position to offer him a bigger contract for 1957. Paul explained that the club was experiencing a financial crunch but that if Flood was smart and continued to work hard, there was room for advancement in the organization. He urged Flood to be patient and to see that his time would eventually come. In the meantime, Flood was offered the same money for 1957 that he earned in 1956: $4,000, take it or leave it. He signed, and his unsentimental education in the world of baseball contract negotiations had begun.

Flood's first year in professional baseball had left him drained as well as disillusioned. Still, when the Reds sent him to the Dominican Republic winter league to continue his seasoning—standard practice with promising young players—he was obliged to go. However, Flood didn't have much pep left in him at that point, and he was cut and sent home after only a few weeks. He was too exhausted to care how this would look on his resume. He was relieved to go home.

Back in Oakland, Flood felt rejuvenated in the presence of his family and George Powles. In their company, Flood felt like somebody. He worked out with Powles's teams that winter and was reminded of his strengths as a player. The following spring, Cincinnati promoted Flood to the Savannah club of the Class A South Atlantic League. Georgia was rife with racial tension at that moment because of school desegregation, and it was obvious to Flood that he would be in for another long season.

At least not all of Flood's white teammates that year were unfeeling. Buddy Gilbert was a sympathetic and good-natured outfielder from Tennessee. When he was seven years old, Gilbert was on a playground with his mother when he casually remarked to her, "Hey, look at that fat nigger over there." Gilbert's mother swiftly slapped him in the head and told him that that word was unacceptable—the Gilberts were no bigots. By the time he played with Flood, Gilbert was genuinely disturbed at the abuse the black players received. While on road trips, he brought black players like Flood and Leo Cardenas (a Cuban who spoke practically no English) meals on the bus, so that they wouldn't have to stand at the back door of the kitchen like beggars. Flood appreciated the gesture and felt badly for Gilbert, who was ashamed that he was powerless to change this situation.

Apart from Gilbert, Flood continued to experience the same sort racism he had endured the previous season. In those days, a team's uniforms would be sent out to cleaned between games of a double header. One on occasion, in the middle of the summer, Flood's team had finished the first game. Along with the other players, Flood tossed his dirty uniform in a pile on the locker room floor. A moment later, the clubhouse manager let out a shriek. When Flood turned around, he saw the man lifting his uniform from the pile with a stick as if it were contaminated. The uniform was removed and sent out separately to a black cleaner. Flood, who was forced to change in a sweltering hot shack just outside of the locker room, had to sit alone, naked, for an extra hour before his uniform was returned. By the time he got it back, the team had already started the second game.

Overall, though, Flood was not as affected by race-baiting as he had been a year earlier. Tougher, he no longer cried in his room at night. He was a seasoned professional. Flood made the league's All-Star team, collected 170 hits, and batted .299. The Reds needed a third baseman, so Curt was repositioned to the infield. He was amenable to doing whatever it took to get him out of the South and into the major leagues. But he was a butcher at the hot corner and made forty-one errors.

Once again, Flood joined the Reds at the end of the year. Cincinnati had come back to earth some after the previous season. The team wound up in fourth place in 1957. Flood didn't see much playing time, appearing in only three games, but the last one was a milestone for him. On September 25 against the Cubs, Flood entered the game in the fifth inning as a pinch runner for Don Hoak, who had doubled. He crossed home plate for the first time as a big leaguer when the shortstop Roy McMillan tripled to right field. Flood flew out in the sixth inning but got another chance to hit in the ninth. The Reds trailed 7-3 when Jerry Lynch opened the inning with a solo home run to center field. Flood was up next, and he faced twenty-one-year-old Moe Drabowsky, possibly the best pitcher on the Cubs that year. Drabowsky was tiring—he had given up a home run to Frank Robinson in the previous inning—but he needed just three more outs to win the game. However, Flood ended his afternoon when he got his first major league hit, a long home run to left field. That was as close as the Reds would get, and it was the last chance Flood would have to hit that season. But it was quite a way to go out. He had homered in the same game as Robinson. Maybe 1958 would be like the old days in Oakland, after all.

Flood was confident that he would now receive a raise, but Gabe Paul had different ideas. Because Flood had played in a higher league, his statistics were not as lofty as they had been in 1956. While it made sense that his numbers would suffer some against better competition, Paul used Flood's stats against him in negotiations. Not that the Reds were ready to give up on him, Paul said. They were willing to give him another chance. If they put their faith in him, would he

Flood in a publicity shot for the Cincinnati Reds in the spring of 1957. While he would see some action with the Reds toward the end of the season, he would have to wait another year before his major league career began in earnest. (Source: *The Sporting News*)

be willing to try even harder? That wasn't even a question for Flood; of course he would. But hopes for a raise were quickly dashed.

The Reds' third base problem was alleviated when veteran Don Hoak had a productive year. Now the club was more concerned about second base. Johnny Temple had been a good player for several seasons, but the Reds wanted insurance in case he went down with an injury; Flood was their choice. Temple, an extroverted team leader, was known as a player who hustled all of the time, and he expected his teammates to follow suit. He also happened to manage a winter league team in Maracaibo, Venezuela, so Flood was sent abroad to learn how to play second base.

Flood went without a fuss, although he was once again spent from the long season. When he arrived in Venezuela, he contracted dysentery and didn't fully recover for a month. Meanwhile, Temple tried to teach him how to play second, but Flood's talents were not suited for the position—he just wasn't a natural infielder. He had a much easier time learning the language, which he picked up quickly, but was alone in a foreign country and was failing miserably at his new position. Though he wasn't discriminated against because of his color, Flood wasn't exactly welcomed either. At the very least, he gained some perspective of how Leo Cardenas and the Latin players must have felt playing in the States.

While dressing after a game before the winter league season ended, Flood received a telegram from Gabe Paul, informing him that he had been traded to the St. Louis Cardinals. Earlier that year, the Reds had signed Flood's childhood friend, Vada Pinson, whom they believed would be a better player than Flood. The Reds already had Frank Robinson, by now an All-Star, and the thought of an all-black outfield was probably too much for them to consider. Flood was the odd man out.

Flood had trusted Paul and had done everything he was asked to accommodate the organization. Now, without any warning, he was being shipped off. The unforgiving reality of the baseball business, rooted in the reserve system, was becoming clear to him. Though he had no recourse but to accept the trade, Flood promised that he would not permit himself to be traded against his will again. He wondered if things would be worse with the Cardinals, but to his surprise, he was offered a $5,000 contract for 1958, a 25 percent raise.

Flood reported to St. Petersburg, Florida, for his first spring training with the Cardinals, hoping to make the major league roster. The thought of another season playing minor league ball in the South was an unpleasant option, to say the least. On the other hand, even if he made the big league club, playing in St. Louis would present familiar obstacles. Though perhaps not so severely as they did in Georgia or Mississippi, the Jim Crow laws that Flood encountered during his stops in the minor leagues existed in St. Louis, too. What's more, the Cardinals didn't have one black regular on their team. The long road to the major leagues was still paved with obstacles and uncertainty.

Chapter Three
America's Team
(1958–1963)

Until the end of 1957, when the Dodgers and Giants moved from New York City to California, St. Louis was both the westernmost and southernmost city in the major leagues. Through the far-reaching power of radio, the Cardinals were enormously popular throughout the South. Fans from neighboring states in the Midwest and the South followed the team religiously. The Cardinals were the New York Yankees of the nation's heartland—America's Team. Led by stars like Stan Musial, Terry Moore, Red Schoendienst and Enos Slaughter, St. Louis won the championship in 1944 and 1946, but shortly thereafter became a mediocre club. Branch Rickey had established the Cardinals as a perennial power, but when he left to run the Dodgers, the team suffered.

The highlight for St. Louis during their years of decline was Musial, a left fielder who was one of the great hitters of all time. Musial wasn't just the best player on his team; he was the face of the organization. Along with Joe DiMaggio, Ted Williams, and Willie Mays, he was baseball's major star, an icon whose recognition reached beyond the game.

For a long time, the Cardinals didn't even have their own

field. Instead, they rented Sportsman's Park from the St. Louis Browns, an awful team that had been the laughingstock of the American League for years. When the Browns moved to Baltimore to become the Orioles in 1954, the Cardinals suddenly had the archaic park to themselves, though they themselves were on the brink of moving to Milwaukee. Before the team could relocate, however, it was purchased by Anheuser-Busch, a local brewery that made Budweiser beer.

Anheuser-Busch was run by August "Gussie" Busch, who had taken over the family-owned business in 1946 and turned it into the world's largest brewery. Busch was known for his interest in sports and promoted the acquisition as a civic-minded move, a goodwill gesture to the people of St. Louis. However, it was also as shrewd a business decision as he would ever make: In 1953, the Cardinals had three different radio stations that broadcast their games to a huge national following. What better way to advertise Budweiser?

At the start, Busch found running a baseball team more difficult than operating a brewery. In his early years, he tried to buy success by offering to purchase stars like Gil Hodges from the Dodgers, Ernie Banks from the Cubs, and Willie Mays from the Giants, only to discover that they were not for sale. Furthermore, the famed St. Louis farm system was no longer churning out talent as it had during Branch Rickey's heyday. Other organizations now had sophisticated systems of their own; the Cardinals didn't corner the market on minor league talent anymore.

When Busch took over the team, he was alarmed that the Cardinals weren't developing any black players. That didn't make sense to him. After all, many of the people who bought Budweiser were black. Why alienate those customers? It wasn't good business. The first two black players that were signed by the Cardinals on Busch's watch were pitcher Memo Luna and first baseman Tom Alston. Both were signed for $100,000, remarkably high bonuses for black players at the time. Neither player flourished, though: Luna never pitched a full inning for the Cards in the major leagues, and Alston, the first black player in Cardinals history, had just 244 career at-bats.

Busch was impatient with failure. By the winter after the 1957 season, he was already on his third field manager, Fred Hutchinson, and his third general manager, Vaughn "Bing" Devine. A St. Louis native born in 1916, Devine had worked his way up from the bottom of the organization. A cautious, deliberate man by nature, he could only hope that his boss would give him some time to return the Cardinals to respectability.

That year, at baseball's annual winter meetings, Devine was on the outlook for help in center field. In 1957, Ken Boyer, the team's promising young slugger, had been repositioned there from third base, where he'd had his share of difficulties. Boyer tried admirably in the outfield but was even worse off there than he'd been at third, and was heading back to his old position. As the meetings drew to an end, Devine was approached by Gabe Paul. The two worked out a deal that sent three pitchers to the Reds and two outfielders, including Flood, to St. Louis. As it turned out, none of the other four men in the trade lasted very long in the big leagues. But Flood was a different story altogether.

Flood made an immediate impression on his manager, Fred Hutchinson, a former pitcher with the Detroit Tigers. Hutchinson, known as Hutch, had been named the *Sporting News* Manager of the Year in 1957 when the Cardinals surprisingly finished in second place. The Cards weren't an especially talented team, but they hustled and overachieved. Hutch was a straight-shooting, fiery man, known to trash the locker room in a rage when his team lost, but he also fair, and treated his players like adults. If he needed to reprimand a player, he did it in private, never embarrassing him in public or in front of his teammates. The players appreciated Hutch's approach and played hard for him.

Hutch liked what he saw from Flood in the field, but he had concerns about his hitting. Flood was having difficulties adjusting to big league pitching, even in spring training. He was able to use his power in high school and in the low minors, but he was now thoroughly outmatched by big league arms. Flood was facing pitchers who threw hard, and with precision and movement. These pitchers could also throw devastating curveballs and change-ups. Like many eager youngsters, Flood was intent on trying to hit home runs. This made him easy to pitch to: instead of driving an outside pitch to the opposite field for a single, he would either ground it weakly to the left side of the infield or would pop it up in an attempt to hit the ball out of the park.

Among the prospects in camp that season was Bob Gibson, a tall, handsome black pitcher who was experiencing his first spring training. A two-sport athlete from Omaha, Gibson had also played basketball for the Harlem Globetrotters for a time. College-educated—he attended Creighton University—Gibson came late to pitching, as he had been a fine hitter in school. That there was another young black prospect was likely a comfort for Flood, though as it turned out, neither he nor Gibson made the major league club. Both were assigned to one of the Cardinals' best farm teams, located in Omaha. The manager there, Johnny Keane, took a liking to both men, particularly Gibson, who he believed could be a great pitcher.

While Flood may have been disappointed not to start the year with the Cardinals, his time in Omaha was brief. In fifteen games, Flood had fifty-two at bats and hit .340, scoring ten runs. He was quickly promoted to the major league team. This was no late-season call up. Flood had made the big time.

The Cardinals needed help in center field and were willing to give Flood serious consideration.

Flood's first game for the Cards came on May 2, 1958 in Sportsman's Park—against the Reds, of all teams. A number of familiar faces would greet him that afternoon: the top four batters for the Reds that afternoon were Johnny Temple, Vada Pinson, Frank Robinson, and George Crowe. Flood started in center field and in the top of the second inning saw his first action, running down fly balls by Gus Bell and Ed Bailey for the first two outs of the inning. In the bottom of the second inning, with Gene Green on second base, Flood had his first at bat for St. Louis and was hit by a pitch. Ken Boyer followed and reached on an error, loading the bases. With one out, pitcher Sam Jones singled. Green scored, and when Brooks Lawrence made an error retrieving the throw from the outfield, Flood scored as well. One at bat, one run scored. Later in the game, he doubled. It was by no means a terrible showing. The Cardinals lost the game, but Flood had arrived.

The Cards didn't feel ready to make Flood their everyday center fielder quite yet. He was a part-time player, with the team largely for his defense. When he did not start, he often entered the game in the late innings as a defensive replacement or a pinch runner. However, he was a pleasant surprise to the team offensively. On May 15, he hit his first homer as a Cardinal against the San Francisco Giants. A few weeks later, Flood hit a solo home run off of Warren Spahn, one of the great pitchers of his era, in a 3-2 loss. On June 23, in Pittsburgh, he had a four-hit game in 7-5 St. Louis victory.

On June 24, Flood badly sprained his thumb but remained in the game and, with the Cards trailing 1-0 in the ninth, hit a two-run, game-winning homer to beat the Pirates. Though swinging a bat was difficult, Flood realized that if he sat out he could find himself back in the minors in no time at all.

Hutch was impressed with Flood's toughness and continued to start him periodically. Flood responded. On July 21, with the Cards and Braves tied at four runs apiece in the top of the fourteenth, he blasted a long, game-winning home run to left field off Lew Burdette.

By August, pitchers around the league adjusted to Flood, taking advantage of his overeagerness and getting him to chase bad pitches out of the strike zone. He struggled mightily for the rest of the summer—in truth, he would not learn how to hit big league pitching consistently for several seasons—and was further frustrated by the lack of guidance offered by the coaching staff. At least he had the opportunity to watch Stan Musial hit. A genial, uncomplicated man, Musial wasn't a rah-rah star who pumped his teammates up and carried on; instead, he was one of the hardest working players on the team, even though he was already one of the greatest hitters of all time. He practiced constantly, and young players could use his work ethic as a source of inspiration. Less useful were his words of wisdom: when Flood once approached him for some hitting advice, he told Flood to find a pitch he could hit and smack the hell out of it.

As the summer wore on, the Cardinals floundered. Their showing in 1957 proved to be a fluke, and they would end the season at 72-82 in fifth place. Flood had a modest campaign, batting .261 in 121 games. He did hit a surprising 10 home runs and 17 doubles but also led the team in strikeouts. Disappointed in the Cardinals' performance, Busch fired Hutchinson as the season came to a close. Truthfully, it was hardly the manager's fault that the team wasn't better, but in the off-season, the Cardinals looked for a new skipper.

It is widely believed that Solly Hemus got the job as manager of the Cardinals because of a letter he had once sent to Gussie Busch. Hemus had been a scrappy infielder for St. Louis, very

At Sportsman's Park, Flood makes a leaping catch of a deep fly ball with two runners on base to end the fifth inning in a game against Philadelphia. In his first year with the Cardinals, Flood quickly established himself as a slick outfielder. (Source: *Associated Press*)

much in the mold of his mentor Eddie Stanky, another retired Cardinal and a favorite of Busch who now worked under Bing Devine. Standing at five foot nine, Hemus had been a Cardinal for seven and a half seasons, surviving with a combination of savvy and hustle. As such, he was a fan favorite. Nicknamed Mighty Mouse, he was an animated, optimistic instigator, needling both opponents and umpires. When Devine's predecessor, Frank Lane, traded him away, Hemus wrote a letter to Busch, thanking him for the chance to be a part of the St. Louis organization. Ballplayers weren't the sort of people who wrote thank-you notes after they were traded, and the letter impressed the Cardinals owner so much that, several years later, he gave Hemus a shot at running his team.

Hemus had no managerial experience, so the move came as a surprise. It also demonstrated Busch's impetuousness. For support, the Cards surrounded the rookie skipper with veteran baseball men: Stanky was named a coach, as were Harry Walker and Johnny Keane, the two strongest managers in the Cardinals minor league system. Should Hemus be unable to handle the job, two excellent replacements were readily available.

Devine also made sure that Hemus had some better players to work with. The Cardinals needed to complement the team's rising star, Ken Boyer, and their legend, Musial. They traded "Strikeout" Sam Jones, the leading winner on the Cardinals staff in 1958, to the Giants for Bill White, the graceful, outspoken first baseman who had given the finger to a racist crowd in the minors. The aging Musial had already been shifted from the outfield to first base to save his legs from wear and tear, but White, in his mid-twenties and about to enter the prime of his career, was too promising to pass up. In San Francisco, he had been stuck behind two other gifted young first basemen, Willie McCovey and Orlando Cepeda. Otherwise, he might already have been a star himself.

Devine also picked up George Crowe as a backup first baseman. This was a minor move on the field but one that had a significant impact in the clubhouse, particularly for the black players. A tall, dignified man, Crowe was a seasoned veteran. Now thirty-eight, he suffered from various leg injuries and was nearing the end of his career, but he was just one year removed from hitting 31 home runs with 92 RBI for the Reds. Though he was quiet, he commanded respect from black and white teammates alike. And as opposed to some other veterans who feared for their jobs, the avuncular Crowe made himself available to younger players. In the absence of attentive coaches, Crowe offered a young black player like Flood the wisdom of his experience. Everything that Flood was going through—both on and off the field—was something that Crowe had lived through himself. He was a through-line from Jackie Robinson to Flood's generation.

Like Bob Gibson, Crowe had been a basketball star before he played baseball. In fact, he was the first black kid ever to play for his high school team and had been named Indiana's first "Mr. Basketball" after his senior year. The school didn't even have a baseball team; Crowe played softball instead. When he graduated, Crowe became the first black student to live on the campus of the University of Indianapolis. Afterward, he played for a professional barnstorming basketball team called the Los Angeles Red Devils, where one of his teammates was none other than Jackie Robinson. Eventually, Crowe played baseball full-time, first in the Negro Leagues, and then for the Boston Braves in the majors. By the time he reached St. Louis, Crowe had seen a lot. Playing two sports for fledgling leagues had proved to be a tough way to make a living.

The White trade turned out well for the Cardinals. He played the majority of his games in left field in 1959 but also spelled Musial at first and provided the Cardinals with offense too, hitting .302. Yet despite his contributions, the Cardinals did not improve and they dropped to seventh place in Solly Hemus's first year, with a record of 71-83.

There were some highlights, though. Back at his natural position of third base, Ken Boyer had another terrific season, batting .309 with 28 home runs and 92 RBI. Meanwhile, Crowe led the National League in pinch hits and was also in charge of the locker room kangaroo court, a time-honored institution of the locker room where players police them-selves. If a player made a careless play during the game, the court might fine him afterwards. Its function was to keep play-ers sharp and humble. It speaks to the kind of respect Crowe commanded that he was in charge of the kangaroo court even though he was black. For the rest of his time with the team, he was known as the Judge.

St. Louis was just emerging from the legal segregation of the late fifties. In fact, White was initially upset when he learned that he had been traded there—it had a reputation as a diffi-cult city for blacks. However, while White had his apprehen-sions, Flood was starting to get his bearings. Though it was indeed not a progressive city, St. Louis was a significantly more accommodating environment than the Deep South had been. Flood could go to jazz clubs and certain restaurants without being hassled. St. Louis was a more sedate version of New Orleans: it had a large black population and a thriving music scene. It was easy for Flood to get an apartment in a black neighborhood. He bought himself a sports car. He was becoming an independent young man.

Early in his time with the Cardinals, Flood got in the habit of grabbing a bite to eat at a walk-up restaurant called Talk of the Town. Walk-ups were precursors to fast food restaurants and were common in black communities at the time. A small kitchen was set behind a glass window, where customers would walk up and order shrimp or burgers. Talk of the Town was located in an area where R&B acts like James Brown and Ray Charles often performed. Ike Turner and Chuck Berry were from St. Louis and also played in the local clubs. Flood enjoyed the nightlife. He liked being out, having a drink and being around people. It offered a respite from pressures he faced every day at the ballpark. Like his parents, Flood loved music, teaching himself how to play the guitar and the ukulele.

Soon Flood began spending extra time lingering over his meal at the walk-up in order to talk to the girl whose parents owned the place. Beverly Collins was a light-skinned girl with high cheekbones and a big, flashing smile. She was stunning. Her parents did well for themselves and were prominent members of the local black community. Though she was only eighteen, Beverly was married when Flood met her and had two children—a young girl, Debbie, and a boy, Gary. Collins's husband, Earl Thomas, had been a good high school football player but hung out with the street crowd and was a hustler. The couple was in a distressed state when Beverly met Flood. Thomas stayed away for days at a time and was completely unreliable. Flood, on the other hand, had a good job and a promising future. Beverly was a bright young woman from a good family, struggling to take care of two young kids while her husband was out on the streets all day. She found Flood appealing, and it's easy to imagine why.

Flood and Beverly' grew romantic. Their relationship was passionate, and they quickly became serious about one another. Flood cared for Beverly's two children and wanted to marry her, so she divorced Thomas, and at the end of the season, the two went to Mexico and married. The following year, Flood adopted Debbie and Gary.

Though Flood found happiness with Beverly and her kids, 1959 was a difficult year for him on the field. Hemus did not have the patience to let him work through his offensive troubles, so Flood was benched while Hemus tried a variety of different players in center field—mediocre talents like Gino Cimoli, Don Taussig, and Don Landrum—trying to find the right combination of hitting and fielding. Flood was used sparingly and, as a young player struggling to adjust to major league pitching, he found his part-time status particularly upsetting. It was hard to improve without getting an opportunity to play regularly, but when he did get an occasional start, he floundered, overanxious as he was to prove himself. It was a vicious cycle. Hemus simply didn't believe in him, and Flood's performance did nothing to change his impression. It seemed almost emblematic that Flood was forced to give up his uniform number when veteran pitcher Marv Grissom, a white player with seniority, claimed Flood's 42. (As it turned out, Grissom would pitch only three games for St. Louis, but Flood stayed with his new number, 21—presumably chosen because it was half of his old number.)

Without the confidence of his manager or any assurance of consistent playing time, Flood began to doubt himself. What was he doing wrong? Why didn't Hemus like him? It's unclear whether Hemus had anything personal against Flood, but the situation was nerve-racking for Flood, who had enjoyed a great relationship with George Powles and a good one with Fred Hutchinson, too. His stress led to insomnia and chronic indigestion. He also smoked many cigarettes a day.

It could not have helped Flood's self-esteem that Vada Pinson played remarkably well in his first full year with the Reds. Just twenty years old, Pinson batted .316, collecting 205 hits with 47 doubles and 20 home runs. He also scored an incredible 131 runs. It appeared as if the Reds had made the right trade.

Nor was it an easy year for Flood's roommate, Bob Gibson, who made the big club in 1959 but not Hemus' starting rotation. While Gibson worked diligently to improve, he was unsuccessful in mop-up work. He would pitch in games only when the team was losing big. Before the end of April, he was sent back down to Omaha. However, on July 30, Gibson returned to St. Louis and made his first big league start. The Cardinals were already well out of contention, but for Gibson the stakes were high. Up 2-0 with the bases loaded and two out in the ninth against the Reds, Johnny Temple stepped to the plate. Gibson fell behind 2-0, and then threw a strike. Temple fouled off the next pitch, evening the count at 2-2. Then he slapped a line drive to short center field. Flood, who had replaced Cimoli to start the ninth inning, sprinted in and made a nice catch to end the game, giving Gibson his first major league win—a shutout.

Gibson, though, pitched inconsistently for the rest of the year—he had a few gems surrounded by some major beatings—and, like Flood, was certain that his manager did not like him. They were not the only players to chafe under Hemus, though. Now in his seventeenth season as a Cardinal, Stan Musial saw his playing time reduced drastically. Musial would collect his three thousandth career hit that summer—he was just the seventh player to reach that milestone—but ended up with the worst batting average of his career.

In all fairness, Hemus was new to managing and had pressures of his own. While that didn't make it easier for young players like Flood and Gibson, Hemus's lack of sensitivity wasn't uncommon for baseball men of his generation—blue-collar guys who had scrapped and clawed for everything that they ever earned in the sport. Moreover, there was a growing generation gap between men like Hemus and the younger players. Increasingly, younger players were better educated, and some had college degrees. Hemus's coarse style was not suited to them. What's more, his attitude toward black players was dubious. Flood believed that Hemus treated him differently than he did white players, and Hemus belittled Gibson, excluding him from pre-game meetings with other pitchers.

One incident cemented Flood and Gibson's feelings about their manager. In a game against the Pirates, Hemus put himself in the lineup to bat against Bennie Daniels. (He was on the roster as a part-time player, not unusual for players-turned-managers during this time.) Daniels, who was black, brushed Hemus back with the first pitch, knocking him to the ground. On the second pitch, Hemus swung and let his bat fly toward the mound. In the late fifties, pitchers threw at the hitters far more frequently than they do now. In turn, if a batter let his bat "accidentally" slip, it wasn't considered an egregious offense. On the third pitch, Daniels plunked Hemus in the back. Hemus shouted something at Daniels as he walked to first, but nobody in the Cardinals dugout managed to hear what he had said.

The following day Hemus called a meeting together in the clubhouse and told the team that he had called Daniels "a black bastard." Flood and the other black players couldn't believe what they were hearing. To them, Hemus had displayed his true colors. It is hard to know the extent of Hemus's bigotry. Racial baiting was part of the game for men of his generation, and he would have likely made a similar remark had the pitcher been Polish—or Italian or Irish. But for Flood and Gibson, the remark went deeper than gamesmanship. At first, they had been frustrated with Hemus's judgment as a manager; now they despised him as a man.

On February 1, 1960, four black college students from the North Carolina Agricultural and Technical College engaged in a nonviolent protest of the "separate but equal" Southern codes at a Woolworth's lunch counter in Greensboro, North Carolina. They simply wanted to sit at the same counter where white people sat and be accorded the same service. They did not really expect to be served, but they wished to assert their feelings about the current conditions. They were polite and non-confrontational. Not surprisingly, the students were denied service, but since they weren't doing anything illegal, they couldn't be arrested. They returned the following day with more supporters. Soon after, in cities across the nation, black students—and some white students, too—were participating. The media latched onto the story and it became a phenomenon. Though it was not the first sit-in for desegregation of the twentieth century, it was the most far-reaching and influential one so far. It was a way for young blacks and their white supporters to express their disgust with the Jim Crow South. That they risked taunting, beatings, and incarceration for their beliefs made their protest even more impressive.

Baseball players have always lived in a relatively insulated, self-contained world. Rarely are players given to politics or social causes. This was especially true in 1960. Black players lived a precarious enough existence without jeopardizing their careers by being crusaders. Even still, the budding civil rights movement manifested itself in its own small way at the Cardinals spring training camp in St. Petersburg, Florida. The St. Petersburg Yacht Club held an annual breakfast, "A Salute to Baseball," which was a strictly segregated affair. The event was held for the Cardinals, yet no black players had ever been invited; segregation was still legal in Florida, and the black players lived separately from their white teammates. Bill White was not at all pleased about the slight. Although, in truth, he had no desire to wake up at seven in the morning and actually attend the breakfast, he found his exclusion from it degrading.

White spoke anonymously with Joe Reichler, a writer for the *Associated Press*, who then reported the story, which was subsequently read throughout the country. The piece caused a minor stir. The *St. Louis American*, a black newspaper, called for a boycott of Anheuser-Busch. Gussie Busch in turn threatened the St. Petersburg Baseball Committee that the Cardinals would move their spring training facilities if things didn't change. The team brought a lot of business to St. Petersburg, and the business community was fond of Busch; his birthday was during spring training and he liked to party. Eventually the yacht club relented, succumbing to the power of the dollar.

The following spring, White continued to find issues worthy of protest: this time, it was the separate living and eating facilities for black players, who weren't welcome where their white teammates roomed or ate. To address this matter, a motel owner named Jim Walter offered the team two adjoining area motels, and by the spring of 1962 white players and black players would live in the same quarters. Both Stan Musial and Ken Boyer gave up their private beachfront cottages to join the rest of the team. This unifying gesture on the part of the team's two best players was noteworthy. Boyer in particular was instrumental in helping to bridge the gap between the white players and their black teammates. The Cardinals' integrated motel became something of a tourist attraction. People would stop along the highway just to see black and white ballplayers, with their families, living side by side.

In *Sport* magazine a few years later, White reflected on his protest of the segregated housing: "I can't take credit for ending it, but I did say my piece. I think that all of us in the big league should say and do more, even the fringe players. It sums up to this: a man must say what he thinks is right. People respect him for it."

After the 1959 campaign, Flood spent the winter working out in St. Louis. His size worked against him over the course of a long season, and Flood, who had just turned twenty-two, wanted to build extra strength to help increase his endurance and stamina. Though he didn't fully comprehend why Hemus didn't have faith in him, in the end it didn't matter. He was out to prove Hemus wrong.

As spring training began, Flood was considered the leading candidate for the center field job. Hemus, though, continued to test his alternatives, giving other players an opportunity to win the position. No one was as promising as Flood, however, and it appeared that without a better option, he would get the nod. Then, just before camp broke, Hemus inexplicably made Bill White the starting center fielder. The move defied all logic, surprising White as much as anyone. (He was far too slow to play center.) For Flood, it was another exasperating setback.

The Cards started off the season by losing fifteen of their first twenty-three games. Predictably, White didn't fare well in center and was eventually installed as the everyday first baseman. Flood didn't start a game until May 14 against the Cubs in Chicago. He got some regular playing time through the month of June and performed well offensively. During a ten-game span beginning on June 5, Flood batted .441 and had 15 RBI. In two games against the Reds, he drove in eight, hitting two home runs in the second game.

Defensively, Flood gave the Cardinals pitchers room to relax: through July 28 he had just one error. But he again had difficulties at the plate during the middle of the summer, and went back to playing part-time. Flood ended the year batting .237 in 396 at-bats. The team improved, finishing in third place, yet it was the low point of Flood's career, underscored by Hemus, who told him flat-out at one point during the season, "You'll never make it."

While Flood struggled with his role on the Cardinals, he was increasingly at home in St. Louis. He and his family lived in an apartment building there, and Flood was friendly with the neighborhood kids, playing catch with them and talking to them when he was around. Occasionally, he would bring them balls or bats, too. Donn Johnson, a local boy whose mother had been friends with Beverly's family for years, looked after Gary and Debbie from time to time. Once, Flood and Johnson were sitting on the front stoop of Johnson's house, chatting, when Flood realized that he had to leave to go to the ballpark. "Boy, I gotta go to work," he said. Johnson was struck by Flood's choice of words. He had never heard anyone refer to playing ball as work. His father, a janitor, went to work. Flood was going to play baseball. But Flood, who had a family to support, clearly understood that baseball was a business. For him, there was nothing innocent or sentimental about it anymore.

The 1961 season began in much the same fashion as the previous two. St. Louis management continued to feel Flood had potential, and Bing Devine signed him for $12,500 plus a $1,000 bonus. However, Solly Hemus was still not sold. Don Landrum won the starting assignment in center to begin the year. The Cards also traded for Carl Warwick, who played a few dozen games in center that season; Don Taussig played there too. As usual, Flood came off the bench. While the team may have been looking for the next Willie Mays, a superstar centerfielder who would both dazzle in the field and hit forty home runs, it was neglecting a fine talent in Flood.

One day during the season, when the Cardinals were playing the Giants, Gussie Busch was down on the field during batting practice, where he had a chat with Willie Mays himself. He asked Mays how he could get a player who was remotely as talented as Mays was. Mays told him that he already had one in Curt Flood. Busch had always liked Flood personally, and now the young man had the highest of recommendations. However, Busch did not make a habit of getting involved in on-field decisions.

Johnny Keane, the Cardinals bench coach, told Flood repeatedly that his time would come, but Flood had reached a point where he didn't know if he would ever get a legitimate chance in St. Louis—not after what Hemus had said to him the season before.

After a good showing in 1960, the Cards struggled for much of the first half of the 1961 season. The fans in St. Louis were as fed up with Hemus as his players and they frequently booed Mighty Mouse when he came to the mound to make a pitching change. Eventually, Bing Devine decided that a move needed to be made. In early July, with the team eight games below .500 and fourteen and a half games out of first place, Hemus was fired and replaced with Keane. Keane had managed in the St. Louis system for fourteen years and his teams won five pennants, but he had been consistently passed over when it came to managing the big league team. Seventy games into the 1961 season, he was finally given his shot.

It was the most important moment of Flood's career. Shortly thereafter, Keane gave Flood a chance to win the starting centerfield job for good. He also put Gibson in the starting rotation. As it would turn out, all three men would make the most of their new opportunities and would never look back. Liberated from uncertainty, Flood played the best ball to date. Suddenly, if he had one or two bad games in a row, he knew he wasn't going to be sent to the bench indefinitely. In the first three months of the season, Flood accumulated just ninety at bats and hit well under .300. His numbers jumped dramatically with the increased playing time and job security, as he batted .324 in July, .330 in August, and .360 in September and October.

Flood hadn't been efficiently maximizing his strengths—namely his quick bat speed. Keane and hitting coach Harry Walker encouraged Flood to punch the ball all around the field. Crowe also put in a lot of work with Flood and emphasized that a quick, compact swing, accompanied by a short stride of the legs, would help Flood compensate for his lack of size. Walker suggested that choking up on the bat would help, too. The three of them got Flood to change his approach: he now looked to hit extra base hits in the gaps between the outfielders rather than trying (and most often failing) to hit the ball over the wall.

Flood also started to acquire patience at the plate. Instead of lunging at bad pitches, Flood waited for a pitch he could handle, even if it meant letting a couple of strikes go past him. Musial was able to offer some helpful advice, after all, pointing out the tendencies of opposing pitchers. Flood's confidence in his new approach grew. He was able to make contact more consistently, becoming adept at the hit-and-run and at hitting behind runners. He was becoming a more nuanced hitter, a more effective team player.

While Flood's offense was a major development for the Cardinals in 1961, his stellar fielding was already a given. On August 17 in San Francisco, Flood robbed Hobie Landrith of a game-tying, two-run home run in the eighth inning. After the game, Larry Jackson, the St. Louis pitcher, told *The Sporting News*, "I think I'll take Curt home to Idaho with me after the season to make sure that nothing happens to him." Flood was as close to a sure thing as there was in centerfield.

Gibson didn't enjoy the immediate results that Flood did, but like Flood he was liberated from his ambiguous role under Hemus. Keane was a great believer in Gibson, and the sense of trust was mutual: Keane allowed Gibson to learn and even fail on the job. Gibson was clearly gifted but had not fully matured. He ended the season with a mediocre record of 13-12, and he led the league in walks. But he pitched over two hundred innings for the first time in his career and had the fifth lowest earned run average in the league. He wasn't polished yet, so Keane sent Gibson to Puerto Rico to play winter ball. Gibson didn't fare especially well during the regular season there, but when the playoffs began, he became an ace, going 5-0 while pitching under pressure. The experience gave him a sense of confidence that he had never had before.

After going 33-41 under Solly Hemus, the Cardinals went 47-33 for Johnny Keane. They finished the season in fifth place, certainly another disappointment for Busch, but they were headed in the right direction. After the All-Star game, Flood hit .346 and finished at an impressive .322 for the year. In November, he was rewarded with a $16,000 contract for 1962. He was one of the few Cardinals to get a substantial raise. He wasn't about to let his first taste of success go to his head, but Flood ended the season in a much better place than he had been in when it began.

The National League introduced two new teams in 1962: the New York Metropolitans, soon to be called simply the Mets, and the Houston Colt .45s, who would later be renamed the Astros. The American League had launched two new teams— the Angels and the Senators—the year before. There were now twenty major league teams as the geography of the game continued to widen across the country. The expansion teams were weak, which in theory made them easy targets for the established teams in the league. The schedule also expanded from 154 games to 162.

Keane wasn't expecting Flood to hit .322 again. If he could hit .280, the Cardinals would be happy. Flood also knew from experience that he was in no position to rest on his laurels. "You never figure you have it made," he told reporter Maury Allen in spring training. "I'm happy I had the year I did in 1961. That means that I have to work twice as hard this year." On the other hand, he felt assured that for the first time since he played for George Powles, his manager was behind him. "There's nothing like the security of a job," he said to Allen. "This is the first time I've ever felt important to the team. Like I really belonged."

The Cards got off to a fast start, going 11-4 in April, but both the Dodgers and Giants were excellent teams, and the Cardinals needed to keep it up over the long haul if they wanted to contend for the pennant late into the summer. While they didn't stay that hot for long, they did remain toward the top of the standings until the beginning of July, at which point they went on to lose six games to the fledgling Mets and Colts—who were a dismal 5-40 that month against the rest of the league—effectively knocking the Cards out of the race for the year.

Offensively, the Cardinals were solid, but they led the league in men stranded on base. They seemed unable to get hits in key situations, and it cost them. Bill White and Ken Boyer continued to lead the team, though many fans and writers in St. Louis viewed Boyer's season as a disappointment. He unfairly took the brunt of the criticism for the team's leaving too many runners on base. The team captain was expected to be nothing short of a superstar in the mold of Stan Musial. Both offensively and defensively, he was one of the elite third basemen in the game. He was durable and his production was consistent. He was also as steady and humble off the field as he was productive on it. Still, he was the scapegoat among the Cardinals' critics.

Musial rebounded to have a terrific season, batting .330 as he passed Honus Wagner for the all-time lead in hits for the National League and, later in the summer, moved past Mel Ott for the all-time NL lead in RBI. Though he played regularly, Musial also excelled at pinch-hitting, reaching base safely twelve out of nineteen times, collecting eight hits. For his part, Flood picked up where he had left off in the second half of 1961. He played in 151 games and batted .296 with 30 doubles, 12 homers (which would stand as a career high), 70 RBI, and 99 runs scored. Keane regarded him as the best regular on the team that year. However, a continuing concern for Flood was stamina. He missed several games early in the season with a pulled leg muscle. In late August, he missed eight more with a foot injury and a pulled side muscle. Flood reported to spring training at 165 pounds but was down to 155 by the end of the summer.

Though the pitching was chiefly to blame for the Cardinals demise, Bob Gibson was selected as an All-Star, coming into the break with a 10-6 record. He didn't receive much run support in the second half, and his record suffered as a consequence. Then, in September, Gibson was injured taking batting practice. He tried to step away from an inside pitch and his spike caught in the dirt, fracturing his right ankle and ending his season early. Still, Gibson finished the year with a record of 15-13 and an earned run average of 2.85, making him just one of five NL pitchers with an ERA under 3.00. He had established himself, leading the team with fifteen complete games. His five shutouts gave him a share of the league lead, and he was third in strikeouts behind the Dodger's demolition duo of Sandy Koufax and

Don Drysdale. A year after Flood had done it, Gibson, too, had come into his own.

By now, the Floods had two new children: Curt, Jr., born in 1959, and Shelly, born in 1961. Beverly was active among the players' wives, helping to organize charity events, as well as the annual team picnic held at Gussie Busch's country estate. In addition, in an era when mainstream modeling work was hard for blacks to get, she was light-skinned enough to get work as a model for Anheuser-Busch, doing print ads for Budweiser beer.

The Flood family seemed to be thriving, but in fact the marriage was running into trouble. Ballplayers are like traveling salesmen or entertainers, constantly on the road. What's more, for better or for worse, playing baseball requires a level of concentration and self-absorption that makes it difficult for players to be fully engaged and available for their families. Flood missed any number of important milestones in his children's development because he was on the road. When Flood was home, he was often exhausted, retiring to his room to conserve his energy. He tried to interact with his children whenever possible, but he wasn't always able to connect. He played with them on his time, when he was ready. Debbie, Flood's adopted daughter, later remembered one Halloween when her father made her an elaborate fairy costume. She recalled being upset at the time because it wasn't the outfit she had wanted. It was the one *he* wanted to make for her. "It's too bad I didn't appreciate it, because he put so much care and dedication into making it, and it was really beautiful. But it was about his enjoyment, not mine."

The pressures of raising the children fell on Beverly, who changed their diapers, took them to school, and disciplined them. This situation was especially arduous for her because Gary had been born with a hole in his heart and on numerous occasions had to be hospitalized. He suffered from poor circulation, which caused him to have seizures. There was no telling when he was going to have an episode, so Beverly had to be alert at all times. While Flood was as attentive as possible, caring for Debbie and Gary as if they were his own, his absence created a level of resentment and friction between him and his wife that could not be overcome. They had met at a young age, fallen in love, and gotten married before they were mature adults. Now their marriage began to fail. As she reached her mid-twenties, Beverly was discovering that she wasn't suited to being a ballplayer's wife.

Before the end of the 1962 season, Flood got together with Jim Chambers, his art teacher from junior high, when the Cardinals were playing against the Giants in San Francisco. Trips to the Bay Area were always enjoyable for Flood, as he was able to see his family as well as his mentors Sam Bercovich and George Powles. Chambers was eager to introduce Flood to his cousin, Marion Jorgensen, an older woman who lived with her husband in an Oakland suburb. They were both great admirers of Flood. Initially, he was skeptical about spending an evening with two fans. He liked to spend his free time away from the game, and fans would often bombard him with questions or suggestions. Flood was always willing to sign autographs, but he didn't seek out fans' company away from the ballpark.

Chambers, though, was a trusted friend, so Flood accepted the invitation in spite of his reservations. He didn't know that the evening would be a revelation, one of the most memorable nights of his life. The Jorgensens lived in the Montclair district of the Oakland hills, a middle class suburb. Their home was well decorated and tastefully put together, with a library filled with books and all kinds of interesting artwork and furniture. John Jorgensen was fifty-nine years old. He was Flood's height but gave the impression of being even smaller. He had gray hair and a low, calm voice. He was frank but kind. Marion was a good listener, attentive to whatever Flood said and thoughtful in her responses.

That night, Flood and the Jorgensens talked about politics with great exuberance and passion. Flood was not a full-fledged activist, but he was more than aware of the civil rights movement. Earlier that year, on February 25, a record four thousand people turned out for an NAACP rally in Jackson, Mississippi. Jackie Robinson and the boxer Archie Moore were there, and Flood showed up too. Robinson was trying to get more athletes into the struggle, and Flood was honored to be in the presence of that great man who would be inducted into the Baseball Hall of Fame later that summer.

Now, talking with the Jorgensens, Flood's intellect was engaged as it had never been before. Listening to their take on life made Flood recognize just how little he knew about the world. But instead of feeling insecure or deficient, Flood was stimulated. His curiosity was awakened and he was excited by how much about life he still had to learn. These were not the sort of fans Flood expected at all. He felt as if he were home. It was close to a religious experience for him. This was a vulnerable time for Flood. His marriage was falling apart, and what he observed in Marion and John was a closeness that he lacked with Beverly. After the season, Flood brought Beverly to the Jorgensens', and the older couple spent Thanksgiving with the Floods and their kids at their home in Pomona.

John Jorgensen owned an industrial engraving plant. His was a meticulous craft, designing and engraving industrial

stamping dyes. Jorgensen made a good living but was not propelled by financial success. He took the jobs that pleased him,
once refusing one to create a dye that would have printed a
"U.S. Army" stamp on weapons even though it would have
brought a handsome profit. Jorgensen opposed America's military presence in Vietnam and felt it would be hypocritical for
him to turn a profit from such a commission.

Flood had found another mentor. He went into business
with Jorgensen during the off-season. Jorgensen was a good
teacher, and Flood happily immersed himself in learning the
profession. The partnership was mutually beneficial:
Jorgensen knew the quality of Flood's work was solid, and
Flood felt he would have a vocation after his baseball career
was over. The two would work through the day and then have
dinner together, afterwards playing ukuleles and singing songs
or talking politics deep into the night.

The 1962 Cardinals had been a good team but not an elite
one. This did not sit well with the restless Gussie Busch.
General Manager Bing Devine had yet to produce a winner
for him, and Busch raised the stakes in the off-season when he
hired Branch Rickey as a senior consultant for player development. Whether or not Busch meant this hiring to be a direct
threat to Devine, he clearly wanted to do something to ignite
success, even if it meant creating some friction. Though
Rickey was eighty one years old, he was still energetic, opin-
ionated, and determined. While his title was ambiguous,
Rickey had never been a passive observer, and he told Devine
he had no plans to start. The two clashed almost immediately
when Devine proposed a trade with the Pirates that would
send Julio Gotay and staring pitcher Don Cardwell to
Pittsburgh for their veteran shortstop Dick Groat and relief
pitcher Diomedes Olivo. One of Rickey's credos was that it

was better to trade a player a year too early than a year too late. During his early days with the Cardinals, Rickey had been able to replace veterans with younger, less expensive players because his farm system was so deep. This trade—moving Gotay for the older Groat—defied Rickey's philosophy.

But the game had changed. Rich teams like the Cardinals and Yankees no longer possessed the prosperous farm systems that they once had. Devine, along with Johnny Keane and his coaches, reasoned that the thirty-two-year old Groat, who had been the league's Most Valuable Player two years prior, would solidify the infield. His experience would be invaluable to Julian Javier, a young Dominican second baseman acquired from the Pirates several years earlier. Groat's steady bat would help the team offensively, too. Rickey relented, but Devine knew his future with the team rested on how the trade turned out.

Like Devine, Groat had something to prove. The Pirates believed that his best days were behind him, so he worked out all winter to show them they were wrong. He was not a fast runner or an especially gifted fielder, but he was a heady player who knew how to position himself and maximize his talent. The Cardinals quickly accepted him into the fold; they appreciated his competitiveness. Groat got along with his teammates and frequently partnered up with Gibson for games of bridge against Boyer and White in the locker room.

It was normal on most teams for the black players and white players to keep to themselves, forming cliques that effectively segregated the clubhouse, but the veteran Cardinal players fostered a sense of togetherness. That black players and white players interacted with each other in the clubhouse was a testament to the character of men like Flood, Gibson, Boyer, White, and Groat. Groups of them would eat dinner together after the game, talking baseball for hours. Their families would socialize as well. This was especially poignant in 1963, as race relations around the country became increasingly volatile. In April, Martin Luther King, Jr. led a rally in Birmingham where police set dogs on demonstrators. In June, civil rights activist Medgar Evers was murdered in Mississippi. In September, four black girls died in a church bombing in Birmingham.

One young player who benefited from the diversity of the Cardinals clubhouse was Tim McCarver. Signed by the Cardinals for $75,000 in the late fifties, McCarver had seen only limited duty in three seasons with the team. The son of an Irish policeman, he was a hard-nosed, hot-tempered prospect from Memphis, Tennessee. He let his anger get the best of him at times, but on a team with so much experience, McCarver played with relatively little pressure.

Veterans like Groat policed young players like McCarver shrewdly. For instance, if a rookie performed particularly well and was bragging in the clubhouse after the game, Groat would walk up to the player and ask, "How many hits did you get today?" He would say it loudly enough so that other players would notice, and it was said in a flat, unimpressed manner. The rookie would invariably be at a loss for words. The lesson was a baseball standby: *Don't get too high when you win, and don't get too down when you lose.* The kind of consistency displayed by Flood, Boyer, and White was what being a professional was all about. But Groat would also offer rookies tips on opposing pitchers and how to handle various in-game situations. Flood, too, embraced the younger players, giving them advice on the field and in the locker room.

Bob Gibson, on the other hand, was gruff with McCarver, who was his catcher. Like most white bonus babies, McCarver started out his career earning good money. Like most black players, Gibson was paid very little. It is easy to see how hard feelings could develop. Early on, Gibson and Flood tested McCarver to see what kind of man he was regarding race. Sometimes their tests were pointed, as when Gibson asked him for a sip of his soda one day on the team bus. (After considering the proposition for a moment, McCarver replied, "I'll save you some.") Other times, they were playful, as when the two roommates demonstrated how white people shake a black person's hand, wiping their hands on their pants afterwards—which left all three men laughing. In the end, McCarver, who had a big heart and an open mind, took the opportunity to examine certain less enlightened values he had been raised with.

Going into the 1963 season, the Cardinals were a veteran team balanced with some young talent. Devine acquired George Altman, a power-hitting right fielder from the Cubs, for pitchers Larry Jackson and Lindy McDaniel. It was a gamble but a pattern that the Cardinals had developed under Devine: trade a good pitcher for hitting. The Cardinals had faith in their ability to develop young arms. However, Branch Rickey wasn't convinced that the team would translate its talent into wins. During spring training he told a magazine that the Cardinals would finish no better than fifth. If there hadn't been tension between Ricky and Devine before, there certainly was now.

Flood had not only established himself as the everyday centerfielder; he was, though only twenty-four, one of the veterans on the team. Batting lead-off, he had two hits in the Cardinal's 7-0 opening-day win against the Mets in New York, but he then went ice cold, going hitless in his next eighteen at-bats. A pulled muscle slowed him down, but he refused to take himself out of the lineup. After all those years of uncertainty, Flood had learned not to ever feel too comfortable. He felt that he was one serious injury away from losing the job that he had struggled so hard to earn.

Groat hit after Flood in the batting order. Using a 36–ounce bat, one of the heaviest in the league, he excelled at hitting behind the runner, slapping the ball to the right side of the field. He also helped steady Javier defensively, as the Cardinals infield became the best in the game, with all four players making the All-Star team. Branch Rickey went so far to call them one of the best offensive infields he had ever seen, conceding by implication that the trade for Groat had indeed been a good one.

The Cards were in first place for most of June but then slumped badly, losing eight consecutive games at one point and finishing the first half of the year in fourth. Still, they were the best Cardinal team Flood had been on. Groat played brilliantly, surpassing his MVP season of 1960, and Flood surged too, hitting .325 in the second half after having hit .281 in the first. In Groat, he found a mentor for his offensive game: the shortstop had virtually perfected the hitting approach that Flood was learning for himself.

The Cardinals had fallen all the way down to sixth place by the time they held their annual family picnic on August 12 — a somber affair this year, as Stan Musial announced that he would be retiring at the end of the season. Television trucks were set up, and the print media took notes. An awkward public speaker, Musial nevertheless gave a pep talk to his teammates, trying to get them to rally and make it to the World Series once more before he stepped aside.

Perhaps inspired by Musial, the Cardinals went on a spectacular run as the summer came to a close, winning nineteen out of twenty games. Not only did they work their way back into contention, they gave Cardinal fans their first taste of a pennant race since the team had last appeared in the World Series back in 1946. With seventeen games left in the season, the team returned home to St. Louis to start an eleven game home stand. Ten days prior, they had been seven games out and their season had looked over. Now they had revived, and thousands of fans greeted at the airport.

It was the first time Flood had experienced anything like the thrill of a major league pennant race. He was exhilarated, though at times he would break out in a cold sweat when the ball was hit to him in a tense situation. In locker rooms or on planes, Flood drew pictures to keep his mind off the pressure.

The Cardinals trailed the Dodgers by just one game when L.A. came into town for a three-game series on September 13. The score was tied at 1-1 in the ninth inning of the first game when the Dodgers scored twice off Bobby Shantz to win it, 3-1. The following day, Curt Simmons, who had been pitching well, went up against Sandy Koufax, the best pitcher in the game. Koufax tossed a gem, allowing only four hits and throwing a complete game as the Dodgers won, 4-0. L.A.'s lead was now three games, and the Cardinals desperately needed to win the finale in order to keep pace.

Fortunately, St. Louis had Bob Gibson on the mound that day, and he came out firing. He also got some help from his offense. Down 1-0 in the second inning, Flood knocked a two-out single to center field and then scored on a two-run home run by Charlie James. In the following inning, Flood drove in two runners—Boyer and White—with a two-out double to right field. The Cards were up 5-1. The score didn't change until the eighth. With one out, the Dodgers collected a walk and three singles, resulting in two runs against Gibson, knocking him out of the game. They ended the inning by closing the gap to 5-4. Then in the ninth, Dick Nen, a utility player who had just been called up to the major league club, hit a game-tying homer off Ron Taylor, his only hit in eight at bats for the Dodgers that year.

The game went into extra innings. Groat led off the bottom of the tenth with a triple, and the Cards had a golden opportunity to win the game. Unfortunately, they couldn't bring him in, and two more tense scoreless innings ensued. Finally, in the thirteenth, the Dodgers scored an unearned run on an error by Javier and won, 6-5. They went on to win the pennant by six games, with the Cardinals finishing second at 93-69. Their rousing late run saved manager Johnny Keane's job, but the Cardinal players were bitterly disappointed. They had made a valiant effort, but Stan Musial would not make it back to the fall classic.

On the last day of the season, the Cardinals celebrated Musial's final game at Sportsman's Park. Musial had reporters around him from early in the morning. Flood, though, was preoccupied with ending his season with 200 hits. Going into the last game, he was two hits shy. As Flood waited to be rubbed down in the trainer's room before the game, the radio played "Stan the Man," a local hit sung by St. Louis nightclub entertainer Marty Bronson. Flood sang along. Later he had Musial autograph a picture, on which Musial wrote, "A fine player—and a fielder who helped me out the last few years." Flood looked at the inscription and teased the older man, telling him, "I was your wheels the last few years."

After going hitless in his first two at bats, Flood led off the sixth with a double. He added a single before it was all over and had his 200 hits—a major milestone—and finished the year with 34 doubles, 9 triples, 17 stolen bases, and 112 runs scored. He was also awarded a Gold Glove award in recognition of his stellar defensive play. Although the Cardinals were losing one of the game's all-time greats in Musial, they at least had Flood, one of the league's bright young stars. At the age of twenty-five, he was just entering the prime of his career.

Chapter Four
The Championship Years
(1964–1968)

Expectations were high for the Cardinals as they entered the 1964 season. Their late-season surge in 1963 created a legitimate sense of optimism. Now with the team's prize infield intact and the pitching looking strong, the pressure had never been greater for Devine and Keane to produce a winner—especially with Branch Rickey in the wings.

As a ball club, the Cardinals were a tight-knit group, professionals who enjoyed each other's company. In fact, they cracked each other up. Gibson, a terrific mimic, was one of the principal comedians on the team, but perhaps the funniest Cardinal was Bob Uecker, a backup catcher who later went on to a successful career as a broadcaster, actor, and pitchman. Uecker would hold court in the back of the bus or in the locker room and entertain his teammates with imitations of Cardinals announcer Harry Carey.

During the season, McCarver and pitcher Ray Sadecki started a routine. One day, Sadecki showed up in the clubhouse with a Wolfman mask, while McCarver dressed up like a hunchback. This prompted Gibson to wear a Frankenstein mask. The players couldn't get enough of being silly, though this merriment didn't undermine their seriousness on the field.

The Cards needed a sense of humor early on. Through the first half of the 1964 campaign, they were a mediocre, slumping team. The Giants and Dodgers struggled too, as the surprising Philadelphia Phillies jumped out to an early lead. As the June 15 trading deadline neared, Bing Devine knew that he had to make a trade to stir his team up.

Two days before the deadline, as the team was preparing to travel to Houston, Devine received a message to call the Cubs general manager, John Holland. The Cardinals were 28-29, tied with Chicago for seventh place. St. Louis had lost nine of its last twelve games, and fifteen of its last twenty-one overall. Holland knew that Devine had been interested in Chicago's young right fielder, Lou Brock, and said that he'd be willing to part with him—but he needed a starting pitcher in return. As a ballplayer, the left-handed hitting Brock was raw, but he was amazingly fast and surprisingly strong. His primary weapon—speed—went largely unused in the power-hitting Chicago lineup, which preferred a conservative approach on the bases.

Holland told Devine that, in exchange for Brock, he wanted Ernie Broglio, who had won twenty games in 1960 and eighteen in 1963. Devine said he needed to speak to his manager. On the flight to Houston, Devine presented the proposed trade to Keane, whose response was quick and unequivocal: having coveted Brock for some time, he asked Devine what he was waiting for. And so Bing Devine pulled the trigger on what at that point was the most controversial trade of his career. Truthfully, he had little choice but to do something drastic. He knew that his job was on the line.

Keane felt that Brock's speed would be a terrific asset for the team. On the other hand, many of the Cardinals players were suspicious, even resentful, of the deal. Broglio was a proven winner. The Cardinal players liked Devine, but some of them wondered privately if he was acting too rashly. In turn, the Chicago press believed that the Cubs had swindled the Cards. Of course, in the end, it was the Cardinals who got the better of the deal—by a long shot. Given the freedom to run the bases, Brock excelled. He would go on to play fifteen seasons in St. Louis and set the major league record for stolen bases, becoming an offensive force and a Hall-of-Famer.

Brock filled the void in left created by Musial's retirement, but he he couldn't singlehandedly turn the team around. On July 24, the Cards were 47-48 and in eighth place, ten games behind the Phillies. In the weeks that followed, they did begin to improve slowly, led by its starting pitching—in particular Curt Simmons, a veteran, and Sadecki, a much-improved young southpaw—though it didn't look as if any miracle comebacks were in the offing. At least Flood was again more than holding his own. He made the All-Star team for the first time in his career, scoring as a pinch runner as the National League won 7-4 at Shea Stadium, and on August 16, he collected eight consecutive hits in a double-header against the Dodgers, going four-for-four in the first game against the great Sandy Koufax, and following it up by going four-for-five in the nightcap.

Still, modest improvements and personal highlights did little to appease Gussie Busch. He was increasingly perturbed by his team's failures. Finally, on August 17, on a day when the Cardinals beat Houston, 3-1, he replaced Bing Devine with Bob Howsam, who was unquestionably Branch Rickey's man. The Cardinals had a record of 63-55 and were in fifth place, nine games behind the Phillies.

The Cardinal players were taken by surprise. They felt that the team was a product of Devine's hard work and design, and were prepared to resent their new general manager without giving him much of a chance. Howsam turned out to be an easy target for their hard feelings. A conservative man by nature, he was a micro-manager, fond of sending his players memos, mostly concerning their appearance. He wanted a clean-cut look that reflected his military background; no long hair would be tolerated. The Cardinals bristled at the squareness of their new GM.

If the team missed Bing Devine personally, it at least finally started to play up to its potential. By September, the Cards had improved to 80-63 and moved into second place, one game ahead of the Giants and the Reds. It looked, though, as if this was too little too late. When Philadelphia returned home to start a seven game home stand on September 21, it had a six-and-a-half game lead with only twelve games to play.

But one week later, everything had changed. The tired Phillies shockingly dropped seven games in a row, and on Sunday, September 27, Philadelphia was knocked out of first place. The Reds were in first and the Cards were only one and a half back. When the Phillies came to town for a three-game series, the Cards had recaptured the same brand of excitement the team had felt during their late-season winning streak a year earlier. Now, though, they played with a looseness that they didn't have in 1963. Having been so far behind, they played like a team that didn't have anything to lose. The Phillies, on the other hand, had tightened up.

Gibson, who had overcome a poor start to the season, pitched the first game and allowed just five hits through eight innings. The Cards sailed to a 5-1 victory. Cincinnati had the day off. The next day the Cards beat the Phillies again, this time 4-2, while the Pirates blanked the Reds, 2-0. Amazingly, the Cardinals were now tied with the Reds for first place.

The following day, St. Louis handed the Phillies their tenth consecutive loss, winning a sloppy, error-filled game,

8-5. Phillies ace Jim Bunning, pitching on only two days rest for the second time in ten days, was hammered. The Cardinal players got together after the game to listen to the Pirates-Reds game on the radio. It was a nailbiting classic, scoreless after nine innings. The drama continued as the game went on and on. Finally, the Pirates pushed across a run in the top of the sixteenth and held on for a 1-0 win. The Cardinals were alone in first place with just three games left in the year. Better still, the lowly Mets were coming to town, while the Phillies and Reds would play a two-game series in Cincinnati. For St. Louis, the pennant was all but won.

It seemed unlikely that the last-place Mets, already losers of 108 games, would pose any threat to the Cardinals, who had been thriving against the best teams in the leagues for weeks, but after an off-day, they found themselves in a tense, Friday-night game. Gibson pitched brilliantly, but Al Jackson of the Mets was even better, and the Mets pulled out a 1-0 win. Meanwhile, the Phillies came from behind to beat the Reds, 4-3. The Cards remained a half game ahead of the Reds and one and a half in front of the Phillies.

Things got worse for the St. Louis on Saturday. The Reds and Phillies had the day off, while the Mets embarrassed Ray Sadecki and the Cards 15-5. This set the stage for one of the most dramatic finishes in baseball history. There was one game left for each team. The Reds and Cardinals were tied for first with the Phillies trailing by just a game. If the Mets managed to complete their three-game sweep of the Cards and the Phillies pulled out a win against the Reds, there would be an improbable three-way tie to finish the year. League officials scrambled to design a complicated three-way playoff series to determine who in that event would go to the World Series.

In the final game of the season, Curt Simmons wasn't at his best, and after four innings the Mets were ahead, 3-2. Sensing the urgency of the moment, Johnny Keane brought Gibson, working on two days rest, into the game. The scoreboard at Busch Stadium showed that the Phillies were blasting the Reds, ensuring at least a first-place tie for the Cardinals. The team relaxed, and while Gibson labored, the offense scored six runs in the middle innings. Flood added a leadoff homer in the ninth, and St. Louis won 11-5. They were going to the World Series.

Flood had had another noteable season, batting .311, scoring 97 runs, and breaking the 200-hit mark for the second consecutive year, finishing with 211; and for the second year in a row, he would be awarded a Gold Glove for his defensive work. But while he and his teammates had overcome many obstacles in 1964, their biggest, most important test was still to come.

While the Cardinals were playing in the World Series for the first time since 1946, the New York Yankees were making their fifth straight appearance and their fifteenth in the past eighteen years. The team had won it all ten times since 1947, the longest sustained period of excellence in baseball history. In spite of increasing vulnerability—most notably in the frail legs of the great Mickey Mantle—and decreasing popularity, here they were, back in the postseason.

The series started in St. Louis on the afternoon of Wednesday, October 7. The Yankees may not have been what they once were, but during warm-ups they still looked confident—smug, their critics would say. The Cardinals, though, didn't have time to be daunted by their illustrious opponents. Everything had happened so quickly. Flood himself was ecstatic. He was arguably the best defensive center fielder in the game—some said still not quite as good as Willie Mays—and one of the most underrated overall players in the

National League. Now he was about to showcase his skills to the whole country.

As the Cardinals warmed up prior to Game One, Bob Uecker was shagging fly balls in the outfield. Nearby, a Dixieland band was performing. When the band took a break, Uecker wandered over, picked up a tuba, and began trying to catch the fly balls with it. His teammates starting placing bets on how many balls he could catch, cracking up the whole time. The Cardinals were ready to go.

Because Gibson had pitched four innings of relief in the last game of the season, Sadecki started Game One for St. Louis. He squared off against Whitey Ford, who was the greatest big-game pitcher of his era but who had been plagued with arm trouble late in the season. Neither pitcher was especially sharp. Brock singled with one out in the bottom of the first. Groat followed with another base hit, moving Brock to third, and then Boyer flew out to right field. Brock tagged and came home with the first run of the series.

New York was not crisp defensively, but it held a 4-2 lead in the sixth, thanks in part to a two-run homer by their young left fielder Tommy Tresh, when the Cards chased Ford from the game with four runs. The rally included a run-producing triple from Flood on a long fly ball to left field that Tresh lost in the sun. In the end, the Cardinals took the first game, 9-5. Although the Yankees didn't announce it immediately, Ford was in too much pain to continue. His season was over, and the Yankees had lost a major advantage.

On Thursday afternoon, Yankees rookie Mel Stottlemyre started against Gibson in Game Two. The two pitchers had completely contrasting demeanors: Stottlemyre, a gaunt sinker-baller, was a cool, composed performer who showed little emotion on the mound; Gibson, by contrast, glared at hitters as he prepared to throw his array of fastballs and sliders. Unfortunately for the Cardinals, Gibson wasn't at the top of his game. After a fast start in which he struck out six of eight batters, he struggled through the middle innings. The Cards had a brief lead after Flood drove in a run on a ground out, but Stottlemyre cruised after that, and New York won, 8-3.

For Game Three, the two teams moved to Yankee Stadium, the most hallowed field in baseball. The spirit of Babe Ruth, Lou Gehrig, and Joe DiMaggio was very real to Flood and his teammates as they stepped onto the field. As a young black kid growing up following the Oakland Oaks, Flood probably never thought he'd actually play in Yankee Stadium, if he even allowed himself to imagine it. Yet here he was, on the greatest stage in baseball.

Neither of the first two games could have been considered classics, but Game Three was a taut pitchers' duel. Simmons squared off against Jim Bouton, a twenty-five-year old who threw so hard that his hat would fly off of his head after each delivery. The score was tied 1-1 in the bottom of the ninth inning when Simmons was replaced by knuckle-baller Barney Schultz. On his way to the clubhouse shower, he heard a tremendous roar—not a good sound for the Cardinals. Mantle had led off the inning and cranked a first-pitch knuckle ball over the right field fence to end the game and give the Yankees a 2-1 series lead. It was the sixteenth World Series home run of Mantle's career.

With Whitey Ford finished for the season, the Yankees started a promising (if inconsistent) southpaw, Al Downing, in Game Four. The Cards countered with Sadecki, who surrendered hits to the first four batters of the game. Keane, wary after Sadecki's shaky start in Game One, quickly replaced him with Roger Craig. Elston Howard greeted Craig with an RBI single to center, and the Yankees looked ready to blow the game open, but the right-hander escaped further trouble, then struck out the side in the second. He would surrender just one more hit through the fifth inning.

Carl Warwick pinch-hit for Craig to start the top of the sixth and singled to left field. Flood followed with a base hit to right as the Cards tried to mount a rally. After Brock flied out, Groat tapped a tailor-made double play ball to second base, but Bobby Richardson had trouble getting the ball out of his glove. He rushed his throw, and shortstop Phil Linz couldn't hang on to it. Everybody was safe. Instead of an inning-ending double play, the Cardinals had the bases loaded for Ken Boyer, who crushed a dramatic grand slam. A critical fielding error opened the door for St. Louis and they kicked it in. The Cards had the lead and won 4-3. The series was tied once again.

Game Five brought a rematch of the Game Two pitching match-ups. This time, Gibson was on his game, while Stottlemyre wasn't as crisp. Gibson's fastball was blazing and he would end the afternoon with thirteen strikeouts, overwhelming the Yankee hitters. The Cardinals scored a couple of runs in the top of the fifth, and Gibson had a shutout going into the bottom of the ninth. It was the kind of performance that the Cardinals, not to mention the rest of the National League, had become accustomed to.

With just three outs to go, however, Gibson ran into trouble. Mantle reached base to lead off the bottom of the ninth when Groat bobbled his grounder. After Howard struck out, Joe Pepitone smacked a ground ball up the middle. The ball hit Gibson's backside and ricocheted towards third base. Gibson, whose follow-through propelled him toward the first base dugout, changed direction, intuitively grabbed the ball, and, now falling toward the third base dugout, made a side arm throw that barely nailed Pepitone at first base. It was a brilliant defensive play that displayed Gibson's athleticism, and it turned out to be critical, as Tommy Tresh followed with a homer that tied the game instead of winning it.

Bill White led off the top of the tenth. He had been in a rut for the entire series and was desperate to get on base. White worked the count full, fouling off five pitches in the process, and finally walked. He moved to second on Boyer's single and then stole third base with Groat at the plate. Groat hit a ground ball to third and reached first as Boyer was forced at second. McCarver, the Cardinals' best hitter to that point in the series, followed. In the most important at-bat of his young career, McCarver blasted a three run home run to right. Gibson finished the game, pitching ten innings—an accomplishment that has become a rarity in the modern game. The Cardinals grabbed a 3-2 series lead as the two teams returned to St. Louis.

The Cards were one win away from a championship, but the Yankees were not prepared to go down without a fight. It was Simmons versus Bouton again in Game Six. Flood got one hit in three at-bats and scored twice, but Bouton was impressive for a second time. Simmons pitched reasonably well, allowing three runs through six and a third innings, keeping his team in the game. But with the score 3-1 in favor of the Yankees, the Bronx Bombers scored five times off the Cardinals bullpen—Schultz was shelled yet again. The series was going to a seventh and deciding game.

On two days rest, Gibson and Stottlemyre faced each other for the third time in the 1964 World Series. Both men were gassed emotionally, as well as physically, but starting Game Seven of the World Series is what every pitcher dreams about. Ignited by their competitive spirit, running on pure adrenaline, they were both effective in the early innings. Gibson was not as strong as he had been in Game Five, but he kept the Yankees from scoring through the first four.

Boyer led off the bottom of the fourth with a single to center, and Groat followed with a walk. Next, McCarver hit a ground ball to Pepitone at first. The Yankee first baseman pivoted and threw to Linz, who was covering second, to force Groat. Stottlemyre made it to the first base bag in plenty of time to receive the return throw and record the double play, but Linz's throw sailed wide, and Boyer broke for home. Stottlemyre dove for the ball and jammed his right shoulder into the ground, and the Cards had a 1-0 lead.

Mike Shannon—a strapping rookie right fielder who'd been a mid-season call-up—followed with a single; McCarver moved to third. With the light-hitting Dal Maxvill at the plate, the Cardinals tried a piece of daring on the bases: a double steal. Shannon took off for second. Howard's throw was high and Shannon slid in safely. The moment Howard committed to throwing the ball, McCarver broke for the plate. The throw home was late, and the Cards had themselves another run. Maxvill then singled to right and Shannon, barreling toward home, tested the hobbled Mantle. A good throw would have nailed him, but Mantle's peg was off-line and Shannon slid in safely under Howard's lunging tag.

At this point, Stottlemyre's shoulder began to stiffen significantly, and Al Downing replaced him. Lou Brock greeted him with a long home run to lead off the bottom of the fifth, and the Cardinals scored two more runs to increase their lead to 6-0. With Gibson on the hill, the championship looked to be well in hand. But Richardson and Maris started the top of the sixth with back-to-back singles, and Mantle launched a three-run bomb that cut the lead in half. The Cards got one of those runs back on Ken Boyer's solo shot in the bottom of the seventh and led 7-3 going into the ninth inning.

Though Gibson was running on fumes by this point, Keane was not about to take his man Gibson out of the game.

He told Gibson to challenge the hitters, to go right after them. After all, he reasoned, they weren't going to hit four homers off his ace. But while Tresh went down on strikes to lead off the inning, Clete Boyer did follow with a solo home run. Johnny Blanchard, pinch-hitting for the pitcher, then struck out, and the Cards were one out away from a world championship. However, Linz hit *another* solo homer. The shrinking lead was now 7-5.

The Yankees, though, would get no closer. Richardson popped up a rising fastball to Maxvill at second. The ball settled into Maxvill's glove, and the long series and season were finally over. For the first time in eighteen years, the Cardinals were kings of baseball. The players poured champagne and beer on each other in the locker room after the game. They hugged and yelled and carried on. For those who had been together for so long—Flood, Boyer, White, and Gibson—it was particularly sweet. They were a close group of players who believed in one another on and off the field, a fundamentally sound team that played with intelligence and assertiveness. They had taken advantage of the Phillies' collapse and the Yankees' mistakes, earning the right to be called champions.

In the joyous Cardinal celebration after the game, a reporter asked Gibson, who set a World Series record with thirty-one strikeouts and was named Series Most Valuable Player, if he realized that he was only the second black pitcher to win a World Series game. Gibson didn't exactly know how to answer the question, but White was not amused. "It doesn't matter that he's colored," White told reporters. "He's a ballplayer and he's my teammate and that's all that matters. Is he colored? I didn't notice. He could be Japanese or Hawaiian. I don't care. What I care about is does he want to win. I thought we had gotten away from that. I thought we didn't use labels anymore."

While White believed that players shouldn't be judged by the color of their skin, Gibson and Flood would learn that in spite of being champions, they were labeled very clearly. They were still black men living in a bigoted culture. Not long after, Gibson was driving the shiny new sports car that he was given by *Sport* magazine for winning the Series MVP. He was pulled over by the police. Black men driving flashy cars were treated with suspicion. When the policeman recognized Gibson, he let him go without any trouble, but the pitcher was nonetheless furious. He knew that his fame was the only thing that had saved him from being harassed further. Later that winter, a bartender in an Omaha bar refused to serve him a soda. The pitcher spoke with the manager and the bartender finally relented, but when he placed the drink on the bar, Gibson glared at him and walked out of the place.

At the same time, the Floods were trying to rent a home in Alamo, a white suburb about fifteen miles east of Oakland. Though they had separated a year earlier, the couple now was trying to reconcile and keep their marriage together. But just as they were about to sign the papers, the real estate agent tried to talk them out of it. George Finn, the boyfriend of the home's owner, was incensed when he learned that a black family had taken the place. Rumors quickly got back to Flood that should he attempt to move his family in, Finn would be waiting for them with a shotgun.

With the help of Marion Jorgensen, Flood filed suit against the owner in Contra Costa Country Superior Court, asking for a restraining order and $10,000 in damages. Marion coordinated the dealings with the courts and police from her home. At one point, somebody cut her phone lines, but she was not deterred. Superior Judge Richard Arnason granted the restraining order, and the Floods moved into their home, accompanied by U.S. Marshals. Marion came with them, too.

On an otherwise tense day, Flood and his wife Beverley smile by the pool at their new house in Alamo, California. Neighbors stopped by to wish them well, and the local media were present to record the scene. (Source: *Associated Press*)

Photographers and a few reporters were there as well. Flood was now the father of five children. His youngest, Scott, had just been born. There were only a couple of black families in the neighborhood, but Flood was not going to be intimidated by a racist thug. It was a sunny autumn day when they arrived at the house. Several neighbors showed up to offer their support. Word had it that Finn would be lurking, either inside the house or in a van nearby. He was nowhere to be seen, though when the Floods arrived, they discovered that somebody, presumably Finn, had changed the locks to the house. With the help of the police, they broke down the front door. Later a locksmith came to fix and change the rest of the locks.

Outside, Flood spoke to television reporters. Beverly, wearing a checkered bandana and looking ill at ease, was by his side. "The notoriety that undoubtedly comes with being out here will make people aware, if nothing else, that prejudice is not only confined to the southern part of our United States," Flood said. "And if they'd move their mustache, and look under their nose, they would find it right here at home, too. It's unfortunate, but it's certainly the truth."

Finn never did appear, and eventually Flood dropped his suit, but it was not a comfortable time for his family. Beverly was consumed with worry. She didn't have any trouble when she went out by herself or with her mother, who had moved out west, too. They both had blue eyes and fair skin. When she went out with the kids, especially Shelly, who was dark-skinned, it was different. There were only so many times she could stand being called "nigger" at the supermarket.

The children were singled out and picked on by the neighborhood kids. One day, three white teenagers approached Shelly, who was playing with a friend. "We want to see if you're the same color all over," they said to her, and then proceeded to take her clothes off. Shelly eventually ran back to her house crying. Her older sister, Debbie, then eight years old and nobody's fool, found her. Shelly's clothes were on backwards, and she was holding her underwear. With her brother Gary in tow, Debbie stormed out of the house, taking along a bat, signed by Whitey Ford, from her father's display wall. When she found the three boys, Debbie started swinging. She hit one boy in the arm, fracturing it, and gave another a black eye and busted his lip. The third boy ran off before she could get to him. The bat got scratched up on the cement, and there was blood on it by the time she was through.

There would be more scuffles, and the parents of the two beaten boys threatened to sue. Flood was livid. Though Debbie had more than held her own, it was apparent to him that living in Alamo was too stressful for his family. It was not an environment that fostered the kind of reconciliation that he and Beverly hoped to find. Indeed, by the end of the winter, the two of them split up for good.

Bing Devine had watched the Cardinals celebrate their World Series victory from a distance, but he knew that he had played a major role in their championship. Though he'd been deposed, he was voted baseball's Executive of the Year for the second year in a row. The day after the Series was finished, the Cardinals called a press conference. Howsam and Busch waited in front of the press to re-sign Keane. But when Keane joined them he announced that he would not return as manager of the Cardinals in 1965. Instead, he had accepted the job as manager of the Yankees, who had unceremoniously fired Yogi Berra. Keane's actions shocked Busch (though they shouldn't have—Keane had been stewing for months over substantive reports that Busch had met with Leo Durocher about replacing him in August). The sudden, untimely announcement was nothing short of a public relations disaster for the Cardinals owner.

In order to save face, Busch relieved Rickey, perceived to be the cause of much of the front office discord, of his duties. He then hired Red Schoendienst, a longtime favorite in St. Louis, to manage the team. Though Flood and Gibson were distressed to see Keane go, the team had no difficulty adapting to the affable Schoendienst. He had been an outstanding player—a Hall of Fame second baseman—and a bench coach for the team for the past few seasons. Dealing with Bob Howsam continued to be challenging, however. Although the Cards were World Champs, Howsam was a frugal and tough negotiator when renewing contracts that spring. One player later said that Howsam treated them as if they had been a seventh-placed club. Another claimed that Howsam informed the team that their World Series bonuses from 1964—which came from the league, not the team—constituted their raises for 1965. Flood, at least, got a well-deserved increase: his salary went from $23,000 to $35,000; Gibson got a $10,000 bump to $40,000, while Boyer received a $15,000 hike to bring his contract to $65,000, the second highest deal in club history.

The Cards looked to be as good, if not better, than they had been in 1964, as they were starting the season with Brock in left and Mike Shannon in right. From the start, though, things didn't go their way. McCarver missed most of spring training plus the first week of the season due to a broken index finger. What's more, Bob Uecker, McCarver's replacement, suffered a knee injury and went on the disabled list.

It was a sign of things to come. Before the end of the year, Brock, White, Boyer, Javier, and Flood all spent time on the disabled list due to injury. Javier broke his hand in mid-June and didn't return to the team until the beginning of August;

White had a painful hip and jammed right heel and back; and hip injuries plagued Boyer throughout the year, forcing him to wear a corset occasionally. Meanwhile, Flood pulled a thigh muscle chasing down a hit by Ron Fairly of the Dodgers in Los Angeles in late May. He hobbled around for weeks before Schoendienst took him out of the lineup. Flood protested and continued to pinch-hit and come off the bench. But he could not contribute. Finally, Schoendienst had to shut him down completely for several games.

It's an accurate if overused truism in baseball that the most difficult thing for team to do is to repeat as World Champs. The Cards weren't any less willing to face the challenge, but they couldn't stay healthy enough to defend their title with any degree of success. They finished the year in seventh place, one game under .500, as the Dodgers won the pennant and the World Series.

In spite of his injured leg, Flood had another excellent year, leading the team in walks and runs batted in. He fell short of the 200–hit mark, compiling 191, but he hit for more power, as measured by slugging percentage, than in any year of his career. Defensively, of course, he was masterful, winning his third straight Gold Glove. His performance was acknowledged at the end of the year when Flood was given the J. G. Taylor Spink Award as St. Louis Baseball Man of the Year. Lou Brock stole 63 bases and scored 107 runs; Bill White led the team in home runs with 24; and Gibson pitched 299 innings—unheard of in today's game—and won 20 games.

But all was not well. During a losing stretch at the end of June, Howsam publicly criticized his team for not playing as aggressively as it had in 1964. He told *The Sporting News* that at times he "quite frankly felt ashamed of the ball club." Howsam urged Schoendienst to get tougher with his players.

This kind of criticism did not sit well with the Cardinals, who were not losing due to any lack of effort.

Nevertheless, at the end of the season, Howsam sensed a change needed to be made. On the field, the Cardinals were still the team that Bing Devine had assembled, a team Howsam had inherited. In a matter of weeks, that changed dramatically. First, he traded the popular veteran Boyer to the Mets for pitcher Al Jackson and third baseman Charley Smith. Then, one week later, White, Groat, and Uecker were moved to the Phillies for starting pitcher Art Mahaffey, catcher Pat Corrales, and a promising young outfielder, Alex Johnson. The trades rocked the St. Louis fans, who howled in protest, especially at the Boyer deal. Groat was sad to leave St. Louis but wasn't surprised. He could even understand trading Boyer, also a veteran whose best days were behind him. He was dumbfounded, though, that the team would relinquish White in favor of an untested player like Alex Johnson. With the loss of Boyer and White, a huge part of the Cardinals' nucleus was suddenly gone.

White himself was none too pleased. On announcing the trade, Howsam told reporters that he made the move in order for the team to get younger. He said that White was thirty-seven when in fact he was just thirty-two. This slight stung White, who was now headed to Philadelphia, considered one of the toughest cities for black players at the time. He felt that Howsam was punishing him by sending him to the Phillies.

In addition to wanting his team younger, Howsam wanted it quicker too, as the team's new $8 million ballpark, the state-of-the-art Busch Stadium, had bigger outfield dimensions than Sportsman's Park. The Dodgers had achieved success in their expansive new stadium by building their offense around speed and relying on great pitching and solid defense. Howsam thought that this was the model to emulate. He was also working by the Branch Rickey dictum of trading a player perhaps a year too early rather than a year too late. Now only Flood, Gibson, and McCarver remained from the 1959 team. Although they were still young and in the prime of their careers, the stark reality of baseball as a business—imposing and impersonal as their new ballpark—was something they were all keenly aware of.

Nevertheless, Flood was part of Howsam's speed formula and was rewarded for his fine 1965 campaign when he signed a new contract for $45,000—not bad when you consider that the average salary that season was $13,000. Star baseball players did not command the kind of money movie stars received—Audrey Hepburn had earned $1 million in 1964 to star in *My Fair Lady*—but when compared with the average public schoolteacher's salary, which was $6,142 in 1966, they did quite well for themselves.

The Cardinals' offense had considerably less punch with the loss of White and Boyer in the lineup, so Flood was moved down to the third spot in the order. He responded well to start the season, hitting game-winning home runs in back-to-back games against the Mets and Pirates and driving in twelve runs in his first eight games.

Still, it wasn't long before Howsam recognized that the team's lack of power was going to be a problem. On May 8, he traded Ray Sadecki to the San Francisco Giants for first baseman Orlando Cepeda, a formidable RBI man who would fill the void left by White. The Giants had traded White to St. Louis years earlier because of a logjam of talent at first base with Cepeda and Willie McCovey. Now Cepeda effectively replaced White.

Cepeda, a strapping Puerto Rican with a vibrant personality, had fallen out of favor with the Giants' management and would instantly become a focus for opposing teams, lightening the load on the other Cardinal hitters. Once a golden child in San Francisco, he felt that the treatment he received from the Giants was tinged with racial bias. He had never had good knees and seriously injured his right leg in 1961. Though he tried to play through the discomfort, his production suffered and eventually he had to have an operation, and came to bat only thirty-four times in 1965. The Giants felt that he was babying his injury. Black and Latino players often had to fight the stereotype that they didn't play through pain, a ludicrous charge considering that playing under one-year contracts no doubt compelled most players (especially minorities) to play though as much pain as they could possible bear.

The Cardinals were gambling that Cepeda could regain his old form. In the meantime, the team continued to play poorly. Flood hit well during the first month of the season and was selected to the All-Star team for the second time in his career, but after batting .338 through mid-June, he fell into his most prolonged slump since becoming a regular. His old habit of trying to pull the ball returned, and the long season, with its frequent double headers and grueling travel schedule, took a toll on him. Of course, he continued to work hard. Above his locker was a sign that read, *Concentrate*. Cepeda was struck by Flood's dedication and seriousness when it came to the game. He had never encountered a player who prepared as intensely as the Cardinals' center fielder.

Flood did manage to break out of his funk in early September, as the Cards won seven straight games. And while his offense sputtered in 1966, he did win his fourth Gold Glove. His defensive value had grown even greater now playing in Busch Stadium, which had a huge outfield to cover. In fact, his fielding was so good that he didn't make a single error all season long. He went 159 games without a miscue, the most ever for a National League outfielder in one year. In all, Flood handled 396 balls perfectly. However, the team slumped to a sixth-place finish as the Dodgers went to the World Series for the second straight season. Howsam's speed experiment had failed.

Nineteen sixty-five and 1966 were years of political volatility in America. While the civil rights movement had been successful in securing legal advances for African Americans, many blacks felt angrier than ever at the state of affairs. Legal gains were not enough, and frustration turned to rage, which soon translated into violence. In February of 1965, Malcolm X was murdered in New York. That summer riots consumed the Watts ghetto in Los Angeles; a year later, riots also erupted in black sections of Chicago, Brooklyn, and Cleveland. In October 1966, the Black Panther party was formed in Flood's hometown of Oakland. Meanwhile, the United States sent its first combat troops to Vietnam at the beginning of 1965, and by the end of 1966 more than 320,000 American troops were fighting there. The war polarized generations and divided families; the counterculture began to flourish, affecting everything from the way people dressed and wore their hair to the kind of music they listened to and the way they viewed the world.

While the sports world was hardly at the vanguard of political or social change, it was not completely removed from it either. In 1964, Cassius Clay won the heavyweight title and then changed his name to Muhammad Ali. Ali was a member of the Nation of Islam, and he acted unlike any other black athlete in the popular eye. Flood and Gibson had befriended the fighter several years earlier during spring training when Ali, then Clay, was staying at their hotel. Flood liked Clay and found him personable and charismatic. Clay brought Flood and Gibson to a meeting of the Black Muslims, and while

Flood was impressed with the dignity and pride that the Muslims projected, both he and Gibson rejected their anti-white rhetoric. In February 1966, Ali stunned the public when he requested status as a conscientious objector after he was drafted to go to Vietnam. He believed that the war was immoral and refused to join the military. Many people were protesting the war, but Ali was by far the biggest star to take a stand against it.

Other sports may not have featured personalities as brazen as Ali's, though increasingly there were strong, intelligent figures who refused to be subservient. Most of these figures were African Americans. In 1965, the first serious protest by black athletes as a group occurred before the American Football League All-Star game in New Orleans, where a number of black players were refused service in nightclubs and restaurants. These players were good enough to play in the game and bring money into the city, but they couldn't frequent the establishments of their choosing. In response, the twenty-one black players at the game refused to play. Their white colleagues supported them, too, and the All-Star game was moved to Houston and played several days later.

While revolution did not seem imminent in baseball, the owners of the game faced a different sort of challenge when Marvin Miller became the Executive Director of the Players Association in the spring of 1966. Raised in Brooklyn (where he rooted for the Dodgers), Miller had sixteen years of experience with the Steelworkers' Union of America, the largest union in the country, where he had been the chief advisor to its president. He had an extensive background in labor negotiations, having worked for the Labor Department and the National Labor Relations Board.

Formed in 1954, the Players Association was originally designed to protect the pension system that the owners had granted to the players shortly after World War II. However, it was not a union in the conventional sense and did not exist to challenge the foundation of the game's economics. While players of this era may not have liked the reserve clause that bound them to one team indefinitely, most of them were grateful just to be playing in the major leagues—a sentiment reinforced by the owners, the media, and the fans. Instead, the association concerned itself with small details: complaints about travel schedules, field and clubhouse conditions, and hotel accommodations. It was also quite preoccupied with the players' pension fund. Players didn't have any conception that as employees they had a legal right to one. They felt that it was a gift from the owners and that if they rocked the boat too much, the owners could take it away from them on a whim. The owners believed this to be true as well.

The prevailing myth—conceived of by the owners and reinforced by the press—had always been that baseball was not a business but a sport, a game, the national pastime. However, it was slowly becoming evident to players and fans alike that it *was* a business. The relocation of the Dodgers and the Giants from New York to California in the late fifties had underscored that. Although several teams had previously moved, none were considered institutions in the way the Dodgers and Giants had been. Walter O'Malley, owner of the Dodgers, and Harry Stoneham, owner of the Giants, brought Major League Baseball to California because their teams would be more profitable there than they had been in New York. They were maximizing their ability to make money, and neither man had any abiding sense of loyalty to the team's existing fan base.

Robin Roberts, the legendary pitcher for the Phillies, had long been the National League representative for the Players Association. He had a hunch that the emergence of television was going to play a significant role in the future of the game. Television contracts would continue to go up, he reasoned, which would bring more money into the game each year. This was important to the players, as their pension was funded in a 60-40 percent split from the broadcast money received from the All Star Game and the World Series. By 1965, this came to about $1.6 million per season. Roberts feared that the owners would continue to sign bigger television deals and that the players would not be treated fairly with regard to the pension plan. With the current plan due to expire in March 1967, Roberts felt that it behooved the players to hire a full-time negotiator.

Roberts helped form a search committee to appoint a director to handle future dealings with the owners. The obvious (if misguided) choice was Judge Robert Cannon, who had been serving as the public spokesman for the association. Cannon was entirely deferential to the owners, but the players were nonetheless prepared to offer him the job when he squabbled over his contract, leading them to revisit the idea of offering the job to Miller, who was also being considered. After some reflection, Miller agreed to become the executive director of the union if he were voted in by a majority of the baseball players. After his work with the Steelworkers' Union, the small size of the Players Association appealed to him. There were roughly five hundred major leaguers in 1966, and Miller would need to connect with them personally if he was going to be elected. If he was, it would be a daunting challenge to address an industry that was years behind the rest of organized labor in America when it came to workers' rights.

It was obvious to Miller that the players were being horribly exploited. They didn't have the basic rights that other workers took for granted, like the right to choose their employer. In an interview years later, he said:

The players were considered by the owners to be chattel, and they were chattel, and they were handled as chattel. This is the way it always had been. Now that didn't mean that they were whipped or starved, it just meant that they had no rights. When a player played in organized baseball, whether it was in the major leagues or the minor leagues, he had to do exactly as he was told. If he was traded, if he was sold for cash, if he was traded for another player, he had to go wherever they sent him.

In 1966, holding out was virtually the only weapon that a player had; if a player didn't sign his contract, his team could simply renew the previous one under the reserve clause. Still, that didn't deter Sandy Koufax or Don Drysdale, the two pitching stars of the Dodgers, from trying to leverage significant raises for themselves in the spring of 1966. They held a joint holdout in the hopes that they might get management to bow to their wishes: three-year contracts worth one million dollars. Koufax's lawyer served as their agent.

The demands caught the Dodgers' front office off guard. No Dodger had ever been offered a multi-year contract. But what really concerned them, as well as other teams' management, was that there was a third party, an agent, involved. Agents were not yet a factor in baseball and not surprisingly management was vehemently opposed to their presence. Relations between management and the players had long been paternalistic in nature: management assured players that they would be paid what they deserved, and players were expected to fall in line with what they were offered without grousing too much. More often than not, owners underpaid players simply because they knew they could get away with it. Professional agents would obviously make that more difficult.

The Dodgers could not afford to lose either Koufax or Drysdale, but neither could the two pitchers afford to retire from baseball (although they did line up acting jobs, just in case). Eventually, they agreed to one-year deals: Koufax got in excess of $115,000, Drysdale $105,000. The owners had dodged a bullet: Koufax and Drysdale received hefty raises, but the balance of power remained more or less unchanged. And though the Dodgers paid the two players more than they had wanted to, they didn't lose money in the process. O'Malley had allocated a budget of $100,000 in player raises in 1966. That Koufax and Drysdale received as much as they did simply meant less for the rest of the team.

The economic reality was stacked in the owners' favor. In 1946, the minimum player salary was $5,000; in 1966, it was $7,000, just $2,000 more after two decades of economic prosperity and inflation. In addition, the players had no say in how their pension fund was run. There was no collective bargaining, the standard practice by which industries and unions in America negotiated everything from working conditions to salaries and benefits. While Miller was appalled by the basic inequities in the game, he also knew that he would have to proceed cautiously. At the time, a popular image of a union representative was as a heavy-handed thug, a cigar-chomping goon in the mold of Jimmy Hoffa. Elegant and soft-spoken, Miller couldn't have been further from that stereotype. Still, the players didn't know what to expect. Most of them were frightened by the word union. They didn't consider themselves workers in the same sense that those in other industries did. On top of that, each player was aware that he might be blacklisted if he crossed management— buried in the minors by his team or unofficially banished from playing anywhere altogether.

In March 1966, Miller visited the spring training camps of all twenty teams. He was taken aback at how little baseball players knew when it came to their basic rights as people who earned a paycheck. Miller first went to Arizona and was greeted with suspicion, even hostility by the Cubs, Giants, Indians, and Angels. Angels player representative Buck Rodgers blasted him in the papers before even meeting him. (Rodgers later apologized to Miller, admitting that management had pressured him to give Miller a rough time.) Managers, coaches, and trainers were—and still are—a part of the association, and as Miller met with them, some managers tried to disrupt his meetings. They heckled him and charged that he was a fraud sent by labor mobsters to ruin the national pastime. The trip did not go well for Miller: the four teams voted 102 to 17 against him. He didn't receive a single vote from the Giants.

Roberts was alarmed, and he made sure that Miller was received far better when he went to Florida. Upon visiting the Yankees, one of the most conservative teams, Miller told the players about the basic unfairness of the reserve clause. Most players listened with a vacant look in their eyes. Only Jim Bouton said anything. He asked Miller, "If there wasn't a reserve system, wouldn't there be a problem if players could move freely from one team to another? Wouldn't the wealthiest team get all the stars?"

Miller replied, "What would you say about a system which has produced one team that has won thirty pennants and twenty World Series in the past forty-five years?"

Bouton smiled. "You mean, like the Yankees? I never thought about it like that."

In a calm manner, Miller urged the players to think about things that they hadn't thought about before. More importantly, he listened to them and let them speak about their problems. Over time, it became clear to the players that Miller was there to serve them, not the other way around. He was a resounding success in Florida and was elected the first executive director of the Players Association by a vote of 489 to 136. A union was born.

The owners were not pleased at all that a professional union man was in the game. Their relationship with the association was now bound to get adversarial. However, in Miller's first season, the association took only small steps to solidify its grounding. Faced with an immediate task of generating operating funds, Miller secured a licensing deal with Coca Cola to allow players images to appear on the underside of Coke bottle caps. This brought in $60,000 for operating costs. In order to replace the $150,000 gift the owners had previously donated to operate the association, which they withdrew shortly after Miller took over, the union set in place a dues-checking system to support itself: two dollars from each paycheck a player received would go toward running the association.

By the end of 1966, Miller made his first significant move, scrapping the existing pension plan and agreeing to a new three-year deal that went into effect at the end of March 1967. A total of $4.1 million annually went to the fund, up from $1.5 million. More importantly, the new plan was non-contributory: the players would not have to pay for their own pension. There was no revolution overnight in baseball, but the seeds of change had been sown.

If 1966 was a year of change for baseball, it was for Flood as well. It started on a positive note, as he and Tim McCarver were named co-captains of the Cardinals at the end of spring training. But it was a long season: the Cardinals finished in sixth place at 83-79, twelve games behind the Dodgers. Flood slumped horribly, and, on top of that, his divorce to Beverly became final. Whether personal issues were responsible for his performance on the field, it is reasonable to assume that Flood was distracted.

Things got worse in the off-season. On December 15, Flood received word that John Jorgensen—his partner, teacher, and his confidant—had been brutally murdered in their engraving shop. Flood was devastated. He returned to Oakland, consumed with guilt. Why had Jorgensen been in the shop and not he? The police caught the killer several weeks later, but Flood never returned to the engraving shop again. To make matters worse, Johnny Keane died of a heart attack less than one month later. He too had played an integral part in Flood's development.

Perhaps as a way of coping with the death of his two dear friends, Flood threw himself into painting. That spring, he painted a picture of Gussie Busch that featured the Cardinals owner in a white captain's hat and a white shirt. Busch was presented with the picture in St. Petersburg, and he hung it proudly on his yacht. He was so taken by it that he commissioned Flood to paint portraits of his children as well. Soon Flood was inundated with requests, and business began to flourish. The Disney Corporation even expressed interest in his work.

Morale around the Cardinals clubhouse improved in the spring of 1967 after Stan Musial replaced Bob Howsam. Though he had no practical experience for the position, Musial was an icon in St. Louis, and he and Schoendienst made an appealing management team for the players, owner, and fans. Other than Musial, the most significant change for the Cards (and Howsam's last consequential transaction) was the acquisition of outfielder Roger Maris from the Yankees. Maris was a taciturn man from Fargo, North Dakota, who had never enjoyed playing in the glare of the New York spotlight. The Cardinals needed a left-handed power hitter, and Maris was an ideal fit. To make room for him, the Cards moved Mike Shannon to third base.

The Cardinals had a good nucleus for success. The roster was well rounded and younger than the 1964 squad—Maris was the oldest everyday player, and he was just thirty-two. Gibson also had stronger company on the pitching staff, with Ray Washburn, Dick Hughes, Nellie Briles, and Steve Carlton, a cocky, young southpaw with electric stuff, filling out the rotation.

The racial harmony that had existed on the team with White and Boyer remained an essential part of the Cardinals' clubhouse chemistry. Cepeda, boisterous and engaging, was not only the team's best power hitter but its emotional leader as well. He was the life of the locker room, keeping the team loose and upbeat. Even Maris, who had been withdrawn while he played for the Yankees, acclimated himself. Accepted by his new teammates, he flourished in his new surroundings.

The Cardinals got off to a quick start winning their first six games in 1967. They hosted the Giants in St. Louis to start the season, and Gibson, who relished facing San Francisco's ace, Juan Marichal, pitched a shutout as the Cards won 6-0. The team leveled off shortly thereafter and was just 11-7 going into a three-game series against the Cubs starting on May 5. The series was especially significant for Flood: in it, he set the National League record for errorless games by an outfielder with 206. Flood extended the streak to 226 games (and 568 chances) before he finally made an error on June 4 in a game against the Cubs. His record would stand for almost thirty years.

In the process of setting his mark, however, Flood hurt his arm throwing the ball. Then he banged up his shoulder on July 6 when running into the fence in the finale of a tough series against in Reds. While his streak was alive, he'd played through injuries; now he was sent to the bench. Eventually, on July 13, the team put him on the twenty-one-day disabled list.

The Cards were in first place, but two days later they found more trouble. In the first game after the All-Star break,

Gibson pitched against the Pirates in St. Louis. During the fourth inning, Pittsburgh's star Roberto Clemente, who was known as a vicious line-drive hitter, smacked a ball back through the middle. It cracked against Gibson's right leg and made a popping sound loud enough to be heard by fans throughout the stands. When Bob Bauman, the team's trainer, came rushing out to the mound, Gibson told him to put some tape on the leg so he could get back to business. He had a high threshold for pain, but had not yet fully registered the severity of his injury: the line drive had cracked his fibula. He stayed in the game but collapsed three batters later as he delivered a pitch.

Gibson was expected to miss between four and six weeks. The effects of losing their ace in the middle of the summer could mean the difference between the Cardinals winning the pennant and falling out of contention entirely. For Flood and Gibson, being on the DL was not easy. They were accustomed to playing through injuries. It was one thing for a regular like Flood to desire occasional rest but another thing entirely to be forced to be a long-term spectator rather than a participant. He couldn't wait to get back.

Away from the playing field, Marvin Miller continued to develop the Players Association. Dick Moss, a lawyer who, like Miller, was appalled at how the baseball business operated, was hired as the association's general counsel. In response, the owners established the Players Relation Committee, an executive board to handle future negotiations with the association. They hired a New York-based lawyer, John Gaherin, who had extensive experience representing management in industry disputes.

Miller welcomed Gaherin by sending him a series of articles that Dodgers general manager Buzzie Bavasi had written for *Sports Illustrated* earlier that spring. He wanted Gaherin to know what kind of people he was going to be working for. In one article, "Money Makes the Player Go," Bavasi asserted that some players were motivated only by money, absurdly implying that management was driven by some higher purpose. He also described how much he enjoyed the back-and-forth of negotiating, even though he knew exactly what the team was going to give a player before discussions began. He bragged that any tactic he employed was fair game. This included a "fake contract" stunt he pulled on players: if a player wanted to be paid as much as someone else on the team, Bavasi would have his secretary draw up a fake contract for that teammate—at a salary lower than the one the first player deserved and often less than what the teammate was actually earning. He would then conspicuously place the phony contract on his desk, and would prearrange for his secretary to call him in the middle of his negotiations, knowing that the player would be temped to take a peek at it. When Bavasi returned to the room, the player would usually agree to the salary that was supposedly going to his teammate.

"I've pulled that phony contract stunt a dozen times," Bavasi bragged, "and I'll do it every chance I get, because this war of negotiation has no rules."

But if negotiations were a war, they were a one-sided one—so one-sided that Bavasi didn't feel that he compromised anything by revealing his methods to the public. Unwittingly, though, Bavasi's articles strengthened the union's resolve. Miller and Moss distributed copies to clubhouses around the league. While many players were aware of such ploys, they took Bavasi's public boasting as a slap in the face.

Bavasi's article underscored was how critical it was for members of the association to know how their salaries compared, so Miller and Moss had the players submit their salaries to the player representative for their team. The results further angered players. They had been lied to as a matter of course. One Dodger was promised by Bavasi to be the fourth-highest paid player on the team. As it turned out, seven team-mates made more than he did.

Miller's poll revealed that the average major league salary was $19,000. Thirty-three percent of players made under $10,000. Although he was among the higher paid players, Flood was one of a growing number of major leaguers who were becoming conscious of how unfair their industry was. He began to approach Miller after union meetings to learn more about how the system worked. Though Miller was not yet universally embraced, he was steadily gaining more support, especially with thoughtful players like Flood.

While Flood was hurt, the Cardinals had faltered and lost their lead, mainly due to poor pitching. When he returned to action on July 28, he was forced to throw sidearm because of his shoulder, but he was still able to track down balls as usual. He had never had a strong arm anyway, having compensated by always hitting the cutoff man. Now the infielders aided Flood by going just a bit deeper into the outfield to receive his throws.

Offensively, Flood came back strong, batting .433 in his first seventeen games, of which the Cards won thirteen. On August 10, against the contending Giants, Flood had a key hit in a 2-1 win and hit a triple and single in the next game, a 3-2 victory. Brock, who had gone through an early summer drought, regained his form. He was now the premier lead-off hitter and stolen base threat in the league. Cepeda and McCarver were having great offensive seasons, and Briles, Carlton, and Hughes all made major contributions for the pitching staff.

In all, the team played brilliantly after Flood's return, winning twenty-one of twenty-five games against the best teams in the league, putting themselves comfortably in first place. Like the 1964 club, they were extremely good fundamentally and didn't make many mental mistakes. Cepeda, who was given the nickname "Cha Cha," led the team in a call-and-response chant after games in the locker room. He called the team "El Birdos," a nickname coined by third base coach Joe Schultz. Whether they won or lost, Cepeda would pump his teammates up, keeping spirits high.

Gibson returned on September 7 and worked his way back into shape as the Cardinals rolled to the pennant. Meanwhile, the American League entertained a race that was even more fantastic than the one the National League had experienced in 1964. Four teams—the Minnesota Twins, Chicago White Sox, Detroit Tigers, and Boston Red Sox—battled each other feverishly all season long, down to the final day of action, with the Red Sox, a young team playing over its head, the improbable winners.

Boston had long had a reputation as a country-club team, one that was not necessarily devoted to winning. It was also one of the most racist organizations in the game, having been the last major league team to integrate. That began to change when Dick O'Connell took over as general manager at the end of the 1965 season. The 1967 squad had several black players, including a promising rookie outfielder, Reggie Smith, and a power-hitting first baseman, George Scott. The mid-season acquisition of catcher Elston Howard—the first black man to play with the Yankees—was just the kind of move that Boston would not have considered several years earlier.

On the field, Boston's undisputed star was left fielder Carl Yastrzemski, known throughout New England simply as Yaz. Yastrzemski won the Triple Crown, leading the league in batting average, home runs, and runs batted in—only the eleventh man in modern baseball history to achieve that distinction. What made the accomplishment even more impressive was that it was achieved under the pressure of a pennant race. Yastrzemski responded heroically in the clutch. During the crucial final two weeks of the season, Yaz had twenty-three hits in forty-four at bats, including five home runs and sixteen runs batted in. He played stellar defense, and in the final two games against the Minnesota Twins, hit a game-winning home run and went seven-for-eight overall.

The Red Sox had not been in the fall classic since they lost in seven games to the Cardinals in 1946. After the high drama of the pennant race, which concluded in such riveting fashion, the Red Sox fans were revved up for the series, which began in Boston. Like the old Sportsman's Park, Fenway Park in Boston was an old-fashioned facility. The fans were close to the field, a quality that was missing from the newer stadiums. Boston's ace, Jim Lonborg, had pitched the final game of the season and was pushed back to Game Two, so right-hander Jose Santiago had the dubious honor of squaring off against a rested Bob Gibson. Brock led off the first against Santiago with a single, and promptly stole second. The Cardinals could not drive him home, but he led off the third inning and singled again. This time, Brock advanced to third on a double by Flood and scored on a ground out by Maris.

Gibson was sharp, but in the bottom of the third he left a pitch over the heart of the plate to Santiago, and the Boston pitcher lifted a home run into the left field screen. The game remained tied at one until Brock singled to begin the top of the seventh, his fourth hit of the afternoon. He stole second and then Flood, as he had done so often, made sure he advanced to third with a ground out to first base. Another ground out, this one by Maris, plated Brock. It was all the support Gibson needed. He overpowered the Red Sox, scattering six hits, one walk, and striking out ten in a complete game victory.

On an overcast day in New England, Lonborg started the second game. Without delay, he issued a warning to the Cardinals, buzzing a fastball right underneath Brock's chin, knocking him to the ground. In previous seasons, Lonborg, a hard thrower with good control, had a reputation as a pitcher who was tentative about pitching inside, but in 1967 he made a point of being more aggressive, hitting nineteen batters during the regular season. His message to Brock set the stage for a magnificent performance. It rained on and off as Lonborg set down the first nineteen batters of the game before issuing a walk to Flood in the seventh. The Cardinals first hit didn't come until Javier roped a double with two outs in the eighth, which saved them the embarrassment of being no-hit. By then, though, the game was out of reach. Yaz stroked two home runs as the Red Sox won 5-0 to even the series at a game apiece.

The scene shifted to Busch Stadium, where Cardinals fans were wild about El Birdos. Brock led off the bottom of the first with a triple off Gary Bell, and Flood drove him home on a single to center. Shannon hit a two-run homer in the bottom of the second, driving Bell from the game. Nellie Briles, on the other hand, was effective for St. Louis. He allowed two runs on seven hits, pitching a complete game. It was never close, and the Cardinals' 5-2 victory put them up 2-1 in the series.

This was a key victory, because with Gibson back on the mound for Game Four, St. Louis was poised to take command of the series. On a cold, windy day, Brock once again terrorized Boston. He legged out an infield single to start the bottom of the first and moved to second when Flood smacked a base hit to left. Both men came around to score on a Maris double. Santiago didn't make it out of the first this time and, when the inning ended, Gibson was staked to a 4-0 lead. While the Cardinals' ace didn't have the same zip on his pitches as he had had in the first game, his control was excellent, and he pitched a shutout.

The Cardinals were one win away from winning the World Series, but the Red Sox were a team that had thrived under pressure all season long. It was almost as if they were too young to be nervous about how dire their situation was. Plus, they had their ace Lonborg on the hill, and he picked up right where he'd left off in Game Two. In a taut pitchers' duel, Boston held a slim 1-0 lead going into the ninth inning when Elston Howard singled home two more runs, putting the game away. As brilliant as Gibson had been in his two starts, Lonborg had been just as good, if not better, allowing only one run and four hits in eighteen innings.

Back in Boston, the Cards still had to win just one game, and they had the luxury of knowing that Gibson would be ready for a Game Seven if necessary. Hughes started against Red Sox rookie Gary Waslewski in Game Six. It was a daring move by the rookie manager Dick Williams to put an untested pitcher in such a critical spot. Waslewski didn't arrive from the minors until the middle of the summer, but now, in the biggest game of his life, he allowed just two runs and worked into the sixth inning. The Red Sox pulled away with four runs in seventh and felt good about their chances of ending their Impossible Dream season (as it had been dubbed) with a championship.

But the Sox were perhaps a bit too confident. George Scott, Boston's first baseman, predicted in the *Boston Herald*

Traveler, "Gibson won't survive five." Flood responded to Scott by telling teammates, "Gibson will be drunk by five," meaning that, by the fifth, the Cardinals' victory champagne would be as good as uncorked.

Notorious for irascibility before and during games he started, Gibson was suffering from a toothache and was even grouchier than usual on the day of Game Seven. Collectively, the Cardinals badly wanted to beat the cocky young team from the American League, but Gibson wanted to win in particular after Scott's brash prediction. In the end, Game Seven turned out to be a one-sided affair. Working on two days' rest, Lonborg did not have his usually precise control, and the Cardinals hit the ball hard off of him in the early innings. Light-hitting shortstop Dal Maxvill led off the third with a long triple, and, two batters later, Flood singled to center, driving in the first run of the game. He moved to third on a single to right by Maris and scored on a wild pitch. In one inning, the Cardinals had done more damage to the Boston ace than they had managed in Games Two and Five combined. Two innings later, Gibson hit a home run, avenging the one he allowed to Santiago in Game One, and in the sixth, Javier hit a three-run bomb that put the Cardinals ahead 7-1. The Impossible Dream was over. Gibson went the distance, allowing two runs on three hits. He simply powered his way to the end and bullied the Boston hitters in the process, striking out ten. The Red Sox had enjoyed a fantastic ride, but for the second time in four years, it was the Cardinals who were champions. Cepeda once again led El Birdos in post-game cheers as the Cardinals joyously doused each other in champagne.

Gibson's friend, the musician Les McCann, was in the clubhouse after the gane, and he stood on a stool and raised a clenched fist and yelled, "Black Power!" The Cardinals may have been one of the few teams whose white players were not threatened by such a display.

Professionally, Flood was flourishing. In addition to his achievements with the Cardinals, his portrait painting business was thriving. Later in the year, he also began a photography business, which specialized in high school yearbook photos. Flood moved into a modern three-bedroom pad on the nineteenth floor of a residential high-rise in St. Louis. It had a terrace with a fantastic view of Forest Park and the Central West End. Marion Jorgensen moved in with Flood to run his affairs after visiting him and seeing what a mess the place was; she determined that she was needed. Officially his secretary, Jorgensen also served as Flood's business partner and caretaker, providing him with emotional support and comfort.

Flood also invited his brother Carl, recently released from prison after serving time for robbery, to live with him. Flood was protective of his older brother and wanted to keep him off the streets of Oakland. He gave him a salary and a job as a salesman for the portrait business. In spite of his troubled life, Carl was still charming and attractive, and at first he excelled, sometimes landing three or four commissions in one afternoon. His steadiness did not last long, but Flood was too busy playing baseball to notice when Carl's behavior grew erratic.

Although not as popular as Gibson or Brock, Flood was loved by the fans in St. Louis. The press also liked him, and so did Gussie Busch. There would be business opportunities in the town, even after he retired, if Flood played his cards right. But though he and his teammates were given the star treatment, the fact that he was black made it bittersweet. As he would later write in his autobiography, it was uncomfortable receiving cheers upon walking into a restaurant or nightclub when the only other blacks in the place were bussing tables or washing dishes.

Black athletes were treated differently than other blacks, which distressed and angered Flood and Gibson, as did the gap that still existed between what white and black athletes could earn in and out of baseball. Gibson, for instance, was the MVP of the 1967 World Series, and though he had a better experience than he had had after the 1964 series, he made only about $2,500 in speaking engagements and endorsements during the following off-season. Meanwhile, Yastrzemski reportedly earned about ten times as much from various sources—and not because he was more handsome or better spoken than Gibson.

While white stars like Yastrzemski were all but guaranteed work in baseball upon retiring, there were simply no employment opportunities for blacks as coaches, managers, or in the front office. As Gibson told a *Sports Illustrated* writer, "I have to watch out for myself when I'm playing . . . When I quit nobody will come up to me and ask me if I want to be the general manager." Even given this lack of opportunity, such venting carried risks: a black player who expressed outrage at baseball's institutional racism might find himself traded or demoted to the minors, no matter how good he was. When a reporter from a black newspaper approached Flood in spring training to talk about his feelings about race relations, Flood snapped, "Man, put that pen away. The next thing you know I'll be playing in Tulsa."

If black resentment at the existing system mostly remained submerged, there were other arenas in which the racial injustices of the sports industry was being exposed. Harry Edwards, a young black professor of sociology at San Jose State University, had been a track athlete in the California school system in the early mid-sixties. Now Edwards spoke out against a system that increasingly relied on the performance of black athletes while offering blacks no coaching opportunities or management positions. He went so far as to call for all black athletes to protest the coming Olympics, which were to be held later that summer in Mexico City. This put pressure on the individual athletes to take a political stand or not to compete at all.

Bing Devine returned to the Cardinals as general manager when Stan Musial stepped down in December. He wasn't considered a miser like Bob Howsam, yet Flood and Devine went back and forth when discussing Flood's 1968 contract. Flood had made $50,000 in 1967 and was asking for $100,000. Not surprisingly, Devine rejected the sum.

One of the only bargaining chips that players had at the time was the threat of retirement, a strategy Flood now employed. Devine asked him to reconsider, but at first Flood wouldn't back down. However, although Flood had established his own businesses outside of baseball, they would not bring in the kind of money that baseball did. Eventually he settled for $72,000. Had he been a white star like Ken Boyer, he may well have gotten closer to that $100,000 mark.

Flood was only one of several marquee players on a championship team who needed to be compensated, and when all was said and done, only Gibson, Maris, and Cepeda earned more than he did. Collectively, the Cardinals' payroll reached $970,000, the highest in baseball history. As a group, they were rewarded for their success, yet their salaries and the evolving nature of how the sport was perceived by the public would come back to haunt them.

Meanwhile, the Players Association continued to make progress. On February 19, 1968, the first basic agreement ever negotiated in any sport was signed. The agreement would cover the 1968 and 1969 seasons, and it included several important improvements for players. First, the minimum salary was raised to $10,000. At the same time, the maximum pay cut was reduced to 20 percent. Travel conditions improved, as it became mandatory that the players receive first-class travel and hotel accommodations. Players also saw an increase in their meal money and their spring training per diem (known as "Murphy money"). Importantly, the Uniform Players Contract—the standard contract that each player signed—was included in the agreement, meaning that the owners could not make changes to it without the involvement of the union.

But for the players, the most significant portion of the first basic agreement was the installation of a grievance procedure. Though common practice in other industries, it was a big step for baseball. A grievance procedure would be necessary if, for example, a player or the union felt that a team was not honoring a player's contract. A committee of three people would decide on the legitimacy of the complaint: a representative from the union, a representative from the owners, and the commissioner.

The basic fairness of this system was predicated on the notion that the commissioner was a disinterested judge. However, the truth was that the owners handpicked the commissioner and paid him too. Therefore, Miller and the association expected him to side with the owners in any grievance proceedings. Ultimately, what the union sought was to have an impartial arbiter replace the commissioner, but it knew that it had to be patient. The owners weren't about to give up control so readily.

The most significant off-season move the Cardinals made was the rehiring of Devine. The team was still relatively young and healthy, so there wasn't much need for change. Flood's arm had healed, and pitchers Briles and Carlton were both poised to improve. The Cardinals were primed to defend their title.

Only a few months old, 1968 had already proved to be a momentous year. At the end of January, the Tet holiday in Vietnam was accompanied by a horrendous attack by the Viet Cong that resulted in thousands of causalities. This event is believed to have turned the American public against the war, and by the end of March, a beleaguered President Lyndon Johnson announced on national television that he would not seek reelection. Then on April 4, as the baseball season was about to commence, Martin Luther King, Jr. was assassinated in Memphis, Tennessee. The reaction around the country was swift and violent. Riots broke out in more than one hundred cities. King was the spiritual leader of the civil rights movement, and his death was a reminder of the vulnerability and danger minorities faced every day. The baseball season was delayed two days, moved from Monday, April 8 to Wednesday, April 10, as the country mourned King's death. Some teams didn't recognize the tragedy, though: the management of the Detroit Tigers scheduled practice on April 8, infuriating the black players on the team.

Once the season did begin, the Cardinals got off to a good start but then lost eleven out of thirteen games during one stretch in May. Gibson was just 3-5, as the team just couldn't seem to score runs on the day he pitched. Meanwhile, Don Drysdale of the Dodgers was virtually unhittable, on his way to an unmatched fifty-eight consecutive scoreless innings. On June 4, he notched a record-setting sixth straight shutout, beating the Pirates in L.A. That night, Robert Kennedy celebrated his victory in the Democratic Party's California presidential primary at the Ambassador Hotel in Los Angeles. In his speech, Kennedy congratulated Drysdale on his historic achievement. Shortly thereafter, Kennedy was shot and went into a coma. He died two days later.

The two assassinations—first King, then Kennedy—so close to one another rocked the nation. For many Americans, both men had symbolized hope that things would improve. But in fact, as the summer progressed, it seemed as if the foundations of American society were crumbling. Rioting and violence raged in the cities. Left-wing protesters were increasingly raucous and subsequently met with force by the establishment. In August, at the Democratic convention in Chicago, police openly brutalized protesters as the rest of the country watched on television.

The events around the nation affected ballplayers as much as it did anyone else. In June, when Gibson was asked if he felt pressure trying to match Drysdale's recently established shutout record, he said, "I face more pressure every day just being a Negro." He later recalled in his autobiography, *Stranger to the Game*, "Without a doubt, it was an angry point in American history for black people—Dr. King's killing had jolted me; Kennedy's infuriated me—and, without a doubt, I pitched better angry."

Harry Edwards eventually called off the black boycott of the Olympics, though several black athletes, including Lew Alcindor (the future Kareem Abdul Jabbar), refused to participate. The most gripping scene of defiance, though, came when American runners Tommie Smith and John Carlos won the gold and bronze medals respectively in the 200–meter race. When they stepped onto the winner's platform, both men bowed their heads and raised their fists. Neither wore shoes, and each had a black glove on his hand. This gesture of Black Power symbolized that even in victory, some Americans were driven to protest the inequities that existed in American society.

Earlier in the summer, Flood had been commissioned by a calendar company to paint a portrait of Martin Luther King, Jr. Initially he wasn't sure how he felt about the assignment. He had met King on several occasions and revered him; he didn't want his image to be used in a tasteless or exploitive manner. But the company assured Flood that the picture would be presented with dignity, so Flood agreed to do it. The portrait would be one of his best, "more expressive," he later told the *Associated Press*, "because there's more of me in it." The picture was donated to a benefit concert that was held for King in Atlanta that fall. It was eventually reproduced in the tens of thousands.

By the middle of June, the Cardinals had pulled away from the rest of the pack and flat out whipped the league. It wasn't even close. Known as the Year of the Pitcher, 1968 was a season in which teams struggled in historic fashion to score. Runs per game fell to the lowest mark since 1908, and the league batting average was the lowest ever. Amazingly, 21 percent of all games ended in shutouts. Yastrzemski led the American League in hitting with a modest .301 average, and only five players hit .300 or better in the National League that year. Flood, who made the All Star team for the third time, was fifth at .301. He also won a sixth consecutive Gold Glove. As the Cardinals cruised to the pennant, he was riding high when he made the cover of *Sports Illustrated* in August. The caption on the cover read, "Baseball's Best Centerfielder."

While many Cardinals performed up to expectations in 1968, no player exceeded them like Gibson did. He was not only the best pitcher in the game; his season was one of the greatest any pitcher had ever had. After his slow start, he ended the year with a record of 22-9 and a staggering earned run average of 1.12. In those nine losses, the Cardinals scored

Flood with his portrait of Martin Luther King, Jr. Flood deeply admired King and was honored to paint his picture, which would be later reproduced in the tens of thousands.(Source: *Sports Illustrated*)

a total of twelve runs. Had they scored even an average amount in those games, Gibson might have gone unde-feated—or at least won thirty games.

In the American League, Detroit Tiger pitcher Denny McLain, a free-spirited twenty-four-year old right-hander, did win thirty games, the first pitcher to do so since 1934. He ended the season with a remarkable 31-6 record and a 1.96 ERA. Both he and Gibson won both their league's Cy Young and Most Valuable Player awards. McLain was a brash, outgo-ing personality, famous for drinking plentiful amounts of Pepsi, playing a Hammond organ, and flying planes between starts. He loved being a celebrity and mingled with famous Hollywood personalities. At the end of the season, he released a record, *Denny McLain at the Organ,* and made the cover of both *Time* and *Sports Illustrated.*

Like the Cardinals in the National League, the Tigers ran away with the American League pennant. An exciting team with a penchant for come-from-behind wins, they were pow-ered by slugger Willie Horton (who was born and raised in Detroit) and future Hall of Famer Al Kaline. Detroit's potent offensive led the league in home runs and runs scored, which was partly responsible for a dramatic rise in attendance at Tigers Stadium after ticket sales had dropped off precipitously following the race riots of the previous summer. One of the last teams to integrate, the Tigers had never been especially popu-lar in the local black community—black fans often rooted for the opposing team—but now the team, more racially mixed, helped create a bond between white and black residents.

The night before Game One in St. Louis, McLain jammed on his organ late into the night in the lobby of the Sheraton-Jefferson hotel, even dedicating one number, "Sweet Georgia Brown," to Gibson. On the other hand, he also told the papers that the Tigers were going to humiliate the Cardinals. Gibson was not so outspoken. He didn't make statements before a game; he made them during the game, on the field.

Indeed, the Cardinals' ace utterly dominated the Detroit lineup the next afternoon. By the time the Cards scored three runs off McLain in the fourth, Gibson had eight strikeouts. After Brock added a solo home run in the seventh, the only remaining drama was whether Gibson would break the single-game World Series strikeout record, set by Sandy Koufax in 1963. He had fourteen going into the top of the ninth with the meat of the Tigers order due up. Mickey Stanley led off with a single before Gibson struck out Kaline to tie Koufax. Norm Cash was next, and he too went down on strikes. Gibson had set the record. McCarver got up and walked in front of the plate, motioning toward the scoreboard. Gibson hollered at him to throw him the ball: there was still one batter to get. Horton was up, and Gibson struck him out looking on a slider that was headed toward his hip but then broke late and wickedly over the plate. Gibson had mastered the Tigers in a way that they never been mastered before. McLain admitted later that it was the greatest pitching performance he had ever seen.

Although McLain had been terrific in 1968, Maris warned his teammates that the Tigers' best pitcher was really Mickey Lolich. Maris had seen enough of Lolich while still with the Yankees to know how difficult the wily left-hander could be. Sure enough, Lolich allowed only one run off six hits in Game Two, as the Tigers beat up Briles, Carlton, and the Cardinals, 8-1, to even the series as it moved to Detroit.

Fifty-three thousand, six hundred and thirty-four people filled Tiger Stadium for Game Three. Like Fenway, Tiger Stadium was an old urban ballpark with a certain intimacy. The seating went completely around the field, and the upper deck in the outfields hung over the lower deck, making an inviting target for hitters. Earl Wilson, Detroit's starter, faced off against Ray Washburn, and Al Kaline gave the home crowd something to cheer about in the bottom of the third when he smacked a two-run homer to put the Tigers up 2-0. The Cardinals stormed back in the top of the fifth. After Washburn struck out to start the inning, Brock singled to center and stole second base. Flood, who had walked and popped out in two at-bats, roped a double to left, scoring Brock. Tiring, Wilson walked Maris and was then pulled from the game. He was replaced by Pat Dobson, who retired Cepeda but not McCarver, who hit a three-run homer, putting the Cards ahead. Detroit got a run back on a solo home run by second baseman Dick McAuliffe, but Flood led off the top of the seventh with a single to right field and scored, along with Maris, when Cepeda cranked a three-run homer, cementing a 2-1 series lead for St. Louis.

Gibson started Game Four and in damp conditions was his usual stingy self, allowing one run, five hits, and a walk over nine innings. He struck out ten and contributed offensively by hitting a home run. McLain was again lackluster and didn't make it out of the third. Flood singled once in five at-bats, and the Cards bombed the Tigers 10-1. With a commanding three games to one lead, St. Louis felt it had the series in the bag.

José Feliciano, a blind folk musician whose most famous song was a cover of The Doors' "Light My Fire," sang the National Anthem before Game Five—a soulful and unconventional rendition, infuriating as many as he inspired. The one indisputable thing about his version was that it was long. Like most pitchers, Lolich, Detroit's starter, was a man of routine, and his schedule was disrupted as Feliciano's song dragged on. It affected him so much that he wasn't sharp in the first inning. Brock led off and doubled to left. After Javier grounded out, Flood singled to right driving in a run, and then and came around to score when Cepeda homered to left. Before Lolich knew it, he was down 3-0. But the lefty settled down, and his teammates pushed two runs across the board in the bottom of the fourth to make it a one-run game.

The Cardinals threatened again in the top of the fifth. With one out, Brock reached second on a double. Javier then lined a single over the shortstop's head into left field. Because the ball was hit on a line, Brock hesitated for a moment, not wanting to get doubled off at second should the catch have been made. The ball went through to left, directly at a charging Horton. Brock had excellent instincts to go along with his tremendous speed, but the brief hesitation cost him. Horton unleashed a perfect peg that reached the catcher just as Brock arrived. For some reason—perhaps thinking that Horton's throw could never beat him—Brock did not slide and was tagged out. The Cardinals had blown a great chance to extend their lead.

In the bottom of the inning, Lolich looped a base hit to right, which proved to be the start of the Tigers' winning rally. Three more singles and walk resulted in three runs, and the Tigers held on to win 5-3. The mood of the Tiger fans was electric as they watched their team come from behind yet again.

Two days later, back in St. Louis, McLain pitched his best game of the series, scattering nine hits and allowing just one run. It was never much of a contest. Washburn was abused early, and a ten-run third inning for the Tigers made it a laugher. The final was Tigers 13-1, and once again, St. Louis was headed to a seventh game with its ace Gibson.

Of course, this was the kind of pressure situation that Gibson not only was accustomed to but thrived on. The Tigers were surging, but the Cards, who may have been overconfident in Games Five and Six, did not underestimate Detroit now—especially knowing they had to face Lolich. After a night of rain, it was sunny in St. Louis for the last game of the season. Predictably, Gibson came out firing while Lolich carefully worked around trouble. With two outs in the first, Flood singled to center and then stole second. Cepeda worked a walk, but the runners were left stranded when Shannon flied out to right.

The game remained scoreless in the bottom of the sixth when Brock led off with a single. It was time for the Cardinals to make a move, and Brock was generally in the middle of any St. Louis rally. But Lolich, with his tricky, left-handed pick-off move, caught Brock breaking for second, and the Tigers tagged him out trying to steal. Javier followed by hitting the ball squarely but directly at the shortstop Mickey Stanley for the second out. Then Flood reached on an infield hit to keep the inning alive. Yet he too was fooled by Lolich's delivery and was caught stealing. After he was tagged out, Flood swiped at the ground, angrily. The Cardinals' speed, so often their strength, had run them out of another opportunity.

The tension mounted. Gibson was brilliant, retiring twenty of the first twenty-one batters he faced. Then, with two men quickly down in the top of the seventh, he faced the heart of the Tiger order. Norm Cash slapped a singled to right. Horton was next, and he bounced a single through the left side. Two men on and two out for Jim Northrup, an outfielder who had hit twenty-one homers in the regular season. He went after Gibson's first pitch and pounded a long fly ball to centerfield.

Flood's first step was toward the infield. In an instant, he realized that he had misjudged the ball and turned to go back and to his right, where the ball was tailing. But he slipped on the soggy turf. He didn't fall, but that fraction of a second was enough time for Northrup's ball to sail well beyond his outstretched glove. The ball rolled all the way to the wall. By the time he retrieved it and got it back into the infield, both runners had scored and Northrup was at third with a triple. The catcher, Bill Freehan, followed with a double and suddenly, with six outs left in their season, the Cardinals appeared to be doomed.

When the inning ended, Flood walked up to Gibson and said, "I'm sorry. It was my fault."

Gibson replied, "Like hell. It was nobody's fault."

Gibson stayed in the game and allowed another run in the eighth. Mike Shannon hit a solo home run with two outs in the ninth, but it was too little too late: the Tigers won 4-1 and celebrated their championship on the Cardinals' home field. The series had been extremely close, coming down to the last three innings, but something had to give, and it was Flood and the Cardinals.

Nobody felt as bad as Flood did. The fact that he had misplayed Northrup's fly was one of the terrible ironies that sports presents: Arguably the greatest defensive centerfielder in the game had made a mistake in a crucial situation that wound up deciding the World Series. Flood's teammates defended him to reporters in the locker room after the game. Gibson reminded them how many runs Flood had saved Cardinal pitchers over the years. "If Curt Flood can't catch that ball," Gibson said, "nobody can. I'm certainly not going to stand here and blame the best centerfielder in the business. Why couldn't we score any runs off that lefthander? That's the reason we lost."

Maris, who had just played in the last game of his career, sought Flood out and told him, "Curt, I want you to know you're the best damn centerfielder I've ever seen. I'm proud to have played alongside you."

The media was less forgiving. Bob Burnes of the *St. Louis Globe Democrat* callously suggested that the entire team had been done in by their own excessive materialism. The Cardinals had appeared on the cover of *Sports Illustrated*

CURT FLOOD OF ST. LOUIS
BASEBALL'S BEST CENTERFIELDER

In 1968, as St. Louis won its second consecutive National League pennant, *Sports Illustrated* recognized Flood as baseball's premier defensive center fielder. Ironically, Flood's fielding gaffe would play a critical role in the Cardinals' World Series defeat. (Source: *Sports Illustrated*) prior to the World Series, accompanied by a caption that read "The World's Most Expensive Team." In that article, writer William Leggett had written that "some highly placed baseball people believe that by paying [players] so well the Cardinals are undermining the very structure of baseball." The team having lost, local writers like Burnes needed something to latch onto. The fact that Burnes was close friends with Gussie Busch made the article even more dubious. Yet the perception was out there: the Cardinals were overpaid, and they lost as a result. Never mind giving credit to a great Tigers team that never gave up and featured three terrific performances by Mickey Lolich. Someone had to be blamed. It fell on Flood's shoulders for the miscue in centerfield and on the team in general for having the nerve to lose when they were so well paid. It was a disheartening way to end a rousing year for St. Louis. As it turned out, it would also mark the end of the great Cardinals run of the 1960s.

Chapter Five
Taking a Stand
(1969–1972)

The Cardinals did not have long to recuperate after their disappointing World Series. In November, they went on a five-week tour of Japan, playing exhibition games against Japanese teams. In all, the team had been playing baseball and traveling for ten months. Flood decided to vacation in Europe before returning to the United States. He went to Paris and Amsterdam, visiting art museums and strolling through the streets. Next, he made his way through Stockholm and then to Copenhagen, a town that John and Marion Jorgensen had told him that he would adore. Flood fell in love with the city. He felt free there, blissfully anonymous. And although there weren't many black people, Denmark didn't suffer from the kind of racial tension that existed in the States.

One day, Flood found himself lost in the city, so when a pretty woman walked by, Flood stopped her and asked her for directions—a simple enough gesture, but something he never would have done so casually back home. Yet the woman not only told Flood how to get to where he was going, she showed him the way. The two wound up having a drink together in a local bar, where Flood discovered the playful Danish custom of tossing cherries across the room at strangers. For the warm and inviting Danes, it was a way to break the ice and get to know each other. Flood was so enamored with the city that he had the thought of moving there and buying a tavern when his career was over.

When Flood returned to St. Louis, he returned to the complications of his life as well. Carl had begun using hard drugs again. Marion had helped to keep Carl's struggles concealed, most likely because she didn't want Flood to be distracted by his brother. For his part, Flood had been so preoccupied with his own life that he hadn't seen, or more likely hadn't chosen to see his brother's addiction.

In 1969, Major League Baseball was undergoing some drastic changes. In addition to further expansion, a two-tiered playoff format was introduced for the first time in the sport's history. Baseball hoped that the playoffs would bring more fan interest to the game; they were certain to bring more television revenues. The owners also reacted to how far the pendulum had swung in favor of the pitchers, changing the dimensions of the game to increase offense: the pitching mound was lowered from fifteen inches to ten inches, and the size of the strike zone was reduced.

Overseeing all of these changes was a new commissioner, Bowie Kuhn, a lawyer who had previously worked for the owners. Kuhn had been involved in the negotiations for a new pension plan after the World Series in 1968. Not surprisingly, the talks between the two sides were contentious. At the heart of the dispute was not money but power and control. The players' proposal asked that each team increase its contribution to the pension fund by $125 per player, hardly an outlandish request. But the owners wanted to cut the players out of any revenues generated from television money; the players, in turn, felt that they were being tested. By December, ownership made a final proposal to the Players Association, which the players rejected 461 to 6. The association and the owners were engaged in their most bitter dispute to date.

Marvin Miller was certain that the owners were trying to break the union, so it was imperative that the players remain unified. While in the past lone players had had little recourse during negotiations, the players as a whole could now, with the support of the union, withhold their services: they could strike. Owners applied pressure on certain individuals, and some, like Yastrzemski and Jim Palmer, the star pitcher for the Baltimore Orioles, refused to hold out. But the majority of the players held firm.

The off-season, traditionally full of trades and trade rumors, was now consumed by the business of the game. This was something very new to the baseball public, and as the season approached, the first-year commissioner had a public relations nightmare on his hands. Although he was loyal to the owners, Kuhn realized that with all the changes being implemented in 1969, it would be disastrous for the season to be delayed. Kuhn urged the owners to modify their proposal, which they eventually did. The players' determination to stick together proved to be a powerful weapon, and the events of the winter was a huge success for the association. In addition to a new pension plan, the union and the owners also agreed to establish a joint study committee to explore possible modifications to the reserve system.

The biggest problem for the players was that under the reserve clause they didn't have contracts for the upcoming season. Players and teams began negotiating late in the spring, when most players needed to get back on the field and commence training and conditioning. In 1969, management was able to recoup some of what it had lost in the deal because of the time pressure players were under to sign new contracts quickly.

This wasn't so much a concern for the Cardinals, who had played in their second straight World Series. They were the highest paid team in the sport, and it didn't look as if many of the players were going to take a cut in salary. Flood told the team that if it wanted "the best centerfielder in baseball" it was going to cost $90,000—and not a penny less. On March 2, Flood and five other Cardinals agreed to terms. Gibson became the highest paid player in team history with a $125,000 contract. Flood's $90,000 was the second highest deal on the team.

Despite the commitment the Cards seemed to be making to Flood, his name appeared in trade rumors. Although he was only thirty-one, some questioned whether his peak years were already behind him. Several seasons earlier, Stan Musial had toyed with the idea of trading Flood to Atlanta for outfielder Felipe Alou. Another time, a deal with the Pirates for relief pitcher Al McBean and outfielder Manny Mota was discussed. Then, after the 1968 season, the Cardinals had reportedly come close to sending Flood, Javier, and backup catcher Johnny Edwards to the Astros for their young power-hitter Jimmy Wynn.

Devine denied trying to move Flood. In fact, there were obstacles that made trading the centerfielder problematic even had Devine wanted to. First was Flood's expensive contract. Then there was his disposition: Flood had threatened to retire before and might do so again.

Flood himself was ambivalent. On one hand, he told Maury Allen of the *New York Post*, he didn't have any desire to quit just yet. "I'm making $90,000 now. If I have a good year I can hit $100,000. Three more years at that price and I'll

During spring training before a frustrating 1969 season, a wary-looking Flood stands by the batting cage. Manager Red Schoendienst is in the background with Orlando Cepeda, who would be traded to the Atlanta Braves by opening day. (Source: *The Sporting News*)

be set financially for life. I won't have to work for money. I'll be able to do what I want."

But, Flood continued, he was at that point in his career where the demands of the game were taking a serious toll. "I want to get as far away from baseball as I can," he told Allen. "I am just tired of the struggle, the pressures, the problems of making it, the problems of staying on top, the fighting with the umpires, the struggling for the base hits, the fears, the insecurities."

Ultimately, while Flood was not traded, he sensed his career was entering its last leg. Even though he didn't have to see replays of his Game Seven miscue every night on ESPN (as a player surely would today), he was still haunted by the failure. "It's still here," Flood told Allen, tapping his head.

"Everybody tells me how many times they saw it in the World Series film in slow motion. I see it every day." And after his liberating experience in Copenhagen, Flood was starting to envision a life after baseball.

Devine had a busy off-season regardless, as the Cards underwent an overhaul. Vada Pinson was acquired for the outfield and Bill White returned as a pinch-hitter. Then, on St. Patrick's Day, Cepeda was traded to the Braves for Joe Torre, a talented hitter and prominent player representative, who was out of favor with Paul Richards, Atlanta's anti-union general manager. The trade profoundly disrupted the Cardinals. While Torre was a highly respected player and teammate, Cepeda had been the heart and soul of the team's clubhouse. Mets outfielder Tommie Agee told columnist Dick Young that St. Louis would sorely miss "Cha Cha": "I don't mean he'll hit more than Torre," Agee explained. "[But] he gave a lot of spirit to that club. He wouldn't let them [get] down. He'd come into the clubhouse after a losing game, he'd turn on that record player of his, and take their minds off their troubles. A guy like that means a lot to a club."

Flood believed that management was intent on breaking up the defending National League champs, but as he and the rest of the team absorbed the idea of the Cepeda trade, Flood received more distressing news: Carl had been arrested for trying to rob a jewelry store in downtown St. Louis. After the botched heist, he and his accomplice stole an unmarked police car. They didn't get far. An officer shot out the back tires and the car smashed into a pole. When the officer got to the driver's window, he had his gun pointed at Carl, who said, "Go ahead and shoot." A television cameraman who happened to be on the scene caught the entire episode on film.

An unpleasant spring training intensified five days later when Gussie Busch gathered the team for a talk. Busch invited the board of directors from the Cardinals as well as from his beer company. Members of the press were also in attendance. Busch was furious with the state of affairs in baseball. He wanted to make it clear that he was unhappy with the Players Association and the events of the winter—he had not gotten into baseball to deal with labor disputes. In a long and rambling speech, Busch lectured his players about the business of baseball and, most pointedly, about their responsibilities to the fans:

> Gentlemen, I don't think there is any secret about the fact that I am not a very good loser...[and] personally, I don't react well to ultimatums. I don't mind negotiations—that's how we get together—but ultimatums rub me the wrong way, and I think ultimatums rub the fans the wrong way. If you don't already know it, I can tell you now—from the letters, phone calls and conversations we have had recently—the fans are no longer as sure as they were before about their high regard for the game and the players.

Flood curbed his response when approached by the press after Busch's tirade, but privately he was mortified. The owner was treating his players like a collection of spoiled ingrates when in fact they were a championship team.

The Cardinals were expected to contend for another pennant, yet they got off to a terrible start from which they never fully recovered. They were booed in their home park early in the year and played so poorly that they didn't reach the .500 mark until July 14. By that time, they were eleven games out of first place. They played decently in the second half, propelled by good pitching: Gibson and Carlton combined to be among the best one-two combinations in the league. But Pinson missed more than a month of the season with a hairline fracture. Flood received a deep cut in his right thigh when he was inadvertently spiked by Mets infielder Bud Harrelson. He was given stitches and a tetanus shot, and then had a long, sleepless night. The following morning, the Cardinals held their annual promotional banquet. Flood, exhausted and in pain, did not attend. The team fined him $250 for his absence. Flood protested off the record to reporters, as he would several times as the season progressed. He was just one of several veterans who objected aloud when two rookies were inserted into the middle of the lineup during a series against the expansion Montreal Expos in early September. Schoendienst and Devine were livid; the once-unified Cardinal team had become an embittered bunch. The team finished the season in fourth place, as Flood had a down year (though he still batted a respectable .285 and won another Gold Glove Award); what's more, he was no longer the owner's pet. He was a high-priced and often disgruntled veteran. In the back of his mind, he sensed that his future in St. Louis was suddenly uncertain.

In fact, there was nothing sudden or uncertain about Flood's future. The trade to Philadelphia for slugger Dick Allen had been brewing for weeks. Devine had read newspaper accounts that the Phillies wanted to move Allen, so he contacted their general manager, John Quinn, who confirmed the reports. Devine told him the Cardinals were interested. Quinn then submitted a list of Cardinals that he was interested in. The final offer, with Flood and McCarver as the key players, was submitted at 1:00 A.M. on October 8. The trade was finalized early the next morning. Shortly thereafter, the players involved were notified of the deal. Devine called McCarver, while Toomey was assigned to call Flood and the other players traded—reliever Joe Hoerner and outfielder Byron Browne. The team wanted to inform the players before holding a press conference at 9:30 that morning.

After the call from Toomey, Flood was despondent. "If I had been a foot-shuffling porter, they might have at least given me a pocket watch but all I got was a call from a middle-echelon coffee drinker in the front office," he would write in his autobiography. Flood was well aware of the difficulties Allen had encountered in Philadelphia, where he was the only black star and had a contentious relationship with the press, fans, and management. Flood was not nearly the same kind of disruptive presence, but as with Allen his willingness to voice his displeasure with management had made him undesirable.

Flood told Marion that there was no way that he was going to uproot himself and go to Philadelphia. He would retire first. After the Cardinals held their press conference, Flood spoke with Bing Devine and told him just that. He had no desire to play for the Phillies and no intention of moving his businesses and his life to another part of the country.

Devine remembered Flood's threat to retire during their 1968 contract negotiations, so at first he took Flood's reaction with a grain of salt. Flood told him that he wished that they hadn't reached a mutually agreeable figure back then; it would have spared him his current situation. Devine reminded Flood that he still had several years of good baseball left in him and that he must still like the game or else he wouldn't have continued to play for so long. He felt certain that Flood would change his mind once he had some time to think about it. Later that day, however, Flood issued a statement to the press:

> If I were younger, I certainly would enjoy playing for Philadelphia. But under the circumstances, I have decided to retire from organized baseball, effective today, and remain in St. Louis where I can devote full time to my business interests. I hope all concerned will understand my feelings and reasons for making this decision.

Nobody else involved in the deal protested. Allen, on the contrary, told the *Associated Press* that he was "so glad to be out of [Philadelphia]. Six years in this town is enough for anybody. I'm glad to be away from Quinn and all of them. They treat you like cattle."

Marion suggested to Flood that he could sue. Perhaps he could be deemed a free agent if he brought baseball to court. That would be a long shot, Flood thought. A lawsuit would be expensive and the chances of defeating the Lords of Baseball were slim. Instead, Flood tried to pick up his spirits in Denmark. It was refreshing for him to be there again, away from his life in the United States. Flood mulled his options over. He met a woman in Copenhagen who knew the restaurant business, and they entertained the idea of opening up a nightclub there. Flood could split his time between Copenhagen and St. Louis.

Before coming home, John Quinn contacted Flood, eager to speak with him about playing for the Phillies. Flood said he needed more time to consider what he wanted to do. The two met in St. Louis when Flood returned. Quinn told Flood how the Phillies were changing. They were going to build a new stadium, and the organization was committed to improving. There would be money for Flood. Quinn also promoted the local art scene, telling Flood about exhibits and museums that might interest him. Flood found Quinn to be a considerate man, but didn't think there was anything the general manager could do to change his mind.

Quinn was disappointed, but he had reason to believe that Flood would eventually come around. This wasn't the first time a player had threatened to retire after being traded. Just a year earlier, two players "retired" as a way to earn fatter contracts. The cynical view, held by many sportswriters, was that Flood was simply holding out for more money.

At the same time, Quinn was in an anxious situation. While Allen may have become a problem for the Phillies, he was a legitimate offensive force. Without Flood, the deal, which benefited both teams on paper, would result in a net loss for the Phillies. It behooved Quinn to try to work something out with Flood as quickly as possible.

Flood visited Allan Zerman, a young lawyer who had helped him with the incorporation of his photography business several years earlier. Marion's suggestion—at first dismissible—that he sue baseball had stuck in the back of Flood's mind. Now, he wanted to investigate the possibilities of a lawsuit. The more Flood thought it over, the less upset he was about being traded to the Phillies and the more incensed he became at the entire reserve system.

Flood told Zerman that he didn't want to leave St. Louis. He felt that he had built a life there. He was active in the community and had established himself as a businessman. But if he had to play elsewhere, it certainly wasn't going to be in Philadelphia. Zerman informed Flood that he had three options: He could retire, go to the Phillies, or challenge a team's right to trade a player—in other words, take on the legality of the reserve clause.

While the reserve clause didn't have a direct influence on trades, its indirect effect was profound. If Flood could prove that the reserve clause was illegal, he would be declared a free agent, free to negotiate with any team for his services. Zerman felt the reserve system indeed should have been illegal. He explained that it was only made possible by baseball's exemption from antitrust laws. He also emphasized to Flood that the odds of beating baseball in court were extremely slim. The game was too powerful to be taken down by one player, he reasoned. Flood understood that it would be improbable, maybe even impossible, for him to win in court, but at that moment he was resolute.

It was clear to Flood that the next step was to talk to Marvin Miller. Flood called him in New York and in a calm and rational manner told Miller that he was serious about filing a lawsuit against baseball. Flood said that he had given the matter a lot of thought and there was no way he was going to report to the Phillies. He had spoken with a lawyer and was determined to take baseball to court to test the legality of the reserve clause. Flood wasn't certain that he had a chance of winning, but he was adamant about using this opportunity to take a stand. Miller agreed that he would be fighting an uphill battle. He told Flood that the courts had consistently favored baseball in such issues over the years. But, Miller added, there was a case just after World War II that was settled out of court before it could be appealed in the Supreme Court. This case indicated that baseball's exemption might not continue to hold up, but, as Miller later wrote in his autobiography, Flood would be "foolhardy to bet on it."

Flood asked Miller if the union would be able to help, but Miller was hesitant. He wanted to make sure that this was not simply a case of a dissatisfied player angling for more money. He needed to know if Flood was genuinely committed, and if so, he wanted to make sure Flood understood the ramifications any suit would have on his career, his personal life, the Players Association, and the rest of baseball.

A week later, Flood and Zerman arrived in New York. They met Miller and Dick Moss in the coffee shop of the Summit Hotel on Lexington Avenue in midtown Manhattan. Right off the bat, Flood and Zerman wanted to know what Miller meant about there being "some indication" that the court might go a different way this time.

Miller gave them an informal education on the history of

baseball's antitrust exemption. He told them about the 1922 *Federal Baseball* decision and two subsequent cases that tested that decision. The first concerned George Toolson, a minor leaguer who played in the Yankee farm system. Like many good minor league players during the late forties and early fifties, Toolson was kept in the minors as insurance in case someone on the big league team was injured. As a result, he was not allowed to market his skills to a major league team that might be able to use him. Toolson claimed that baseball violated federal antitrust laws and filed suit. His case made it all the way to the Supreme Court, where the earlier decision of *Federal Baseball* was upheld.

The second case, which led Miller to suggest that the court could possibly rule differently should baseball's exemption again be brought before the Supreme Court, involved Danny Gardella, an outfielder from New York who had joined the New York Giants at the end of World War II. Soon after, in 1946, Gardella became the first player to sign with the upstart Mexican League. Several notable players, including Mickey Owen and Sal Maglie, were also lured by the higher salaries offered by the new league. Later that year, baseball's commissioner, Happy Chandler, banned all players who went to play in the Mexican League for five years. Gardella returned to the states by 1947 but was not allowed to play for a major league team. He protested by taking baseball to court in the fall of 1947, charging the reserve clause was "monopolistic and restrains trade." Frederic Johnson, Gardella's lawyer, argued that baseball was a business engaged in interstate commerce, despite what *Federal Baseball* said. Gardella lost in district court, but the following year, the court of appeals felt that Gardella's suit was worthy of a trial and ruled in his favor.

There was no union at the time, so Gardella was very much on his own. Nevertheless, Commissioner Chandler was worried about what a trial could mean for baseball's exemption, so on June 5, 1949, he allowed all of the ballplayers who played in the Mexican League to be reinstated. Gardella was excluded, but his lawyer convinced him that he would not be able to stand alone against the owners. He didn't have the finances or the clout. On October 8, 1949, Gardella settled out of court and baseball's sacred exemption was safe.

Miller was suggesting to Flood that the court of appeals decision could mean that the courts could reverse *Federal Baseball*. It wasn't likely—overturning a Supreme court decision, no matter how flawed, is rare—but it was possible. In order for the exemption to be overturned, the case would need to be appealed all the way to the Supreme Court, which could take years and would cost a lot of money. Miller also knew that the owners would try to buy Flood off, just as they did with Gardella. "What would you do then?" he asked. Flood replied that he wouldn't accept any buyout. He told Miller that if the Players Association agreed to help support him, he would stick it out until the end.

Miller also told Flood that if he sued baseball, his career would likely be over. "Over the last three years I've learned that the owners are a vindictive group," said Miller. "If you threaten their monopoly they'll see to it that you are through in baseball. "[And] I won't say that they are all racists, but being black isn't going to help." He reminded Flood that Gussie Busch wielded influence in other industries and was a powerful man in St. Louis; he could make life outside of baseball hard for Flood.

Flood took this in and hesitated for a moment but said that he'd find a way to handle it. Miller then added that if there was anything in Flood's life that he would rather not see exposed, he shouldn't go ahead with the suit: the owners would surely find out about it and leak it to the media. Flood thought of

Carl, now in prison for robbery. This gave him pause, but even the risk of publicly exposing his brother didn't faze him.

Miller was impressed by Flood's conviction. After their meeting, he was persuaded that Flood would go ahead with a suit. Pragmatic as always, Miller was concerned primarily about the Players Association. Zerman seemed competent enough, but a large-scale lawsuit like this was over his head. The association would need to provide Flood with the best possible counsel and prepare the best possible case. In the end, Miller didn't want Flood's case to do more harm than good for the association.

Miller and Moss immersed themselves in research. They studied the antitrust suits brought against the football, boxing, and theater industries. All three had had cases that reached the Supreme Court since the Toolson decision, and all three had been forced to comply with antitrust laws. Baseball was different because *Federal Baseball* had established a legal precedent.

It was only after the player representatives were approached that Miller discovered just how difficult Flood's case was going to be. So few players—so few representatives, even—knew anything about the specifics of the reserve system. Even those who may have been opposed to it in theory didn't really know what it meant. Plus, many of them believed the owners' line that the game would be destroyed without it. Miller and Moss had their work cut out for them.

Before he returned home, Flood met Quinn for dinner at a restaurant in Manhattan. Quinn asked him again if he'd be willing to reconsider his retirement. He offered Flood more than $90,000 in salary and an additional $8,000 in spring training expenses. Combined, Flood's annual pay would be over the coveted $100,000 mark, which would put him in an elite class: it was superstar money. (According to *The Official*

Baseball Guide, a *Sporting News* annual, six players, including Gibson, Yastrzemski, and Frank Robinson, made $125,000 in 1970, with four more in the $100,000 bracket. Flood, while a three-time All-Star, was really a defensive specialist and a high-average singles hitter. He was an excellent player, but not a superstar.) Flood told Quinn that he needed to think about it some more.

While the two men were eating, a woman approached Flood excitedly, mistaking him for Lou Brock. Flood corrected her, introduced himself and Quinn, and without thinking much about it told her that he was not with the Cardinals anymore but with the Phillies. He wasn't trying to mislead Quinn, but the gesture may have given Quinn false hope.

Flood thought about the issues that Miller had raised, talking them over with Marion. She was his dearest friend. Not only did she help oversee his business ventures and personal affairs, she cared for him deeply. She was a second mother to him at a time when Flood did not rely on his own family for counsel. Furthermore, she was a woman who was willing to defend what she thought was right. Marion and Flood went back and forth, discussing his options. If Flood took on the baseball establishment, his career and future in the game would surely be ruined. He stood to lose a considerable amount of money. Beyond that, his reputation could be tarnished: instead of being portrayed as a consummate team player and talented artist by the press, Flood would be construed as a spoiled upstart.

But Flood felt strongly that the reserve clause violated his basic civil rights. He thought of John Jorgensen, who had showed him that principled behavior is crucial to a person's self-worth. Now that Flood had seen for himself the injustice of the reserve system, he was obliged to fight against it. Years later, Flood would tell documentary filmmaker Ken Burns:

I'm a child of the sixties, I'm a man of the sixties. During that period of time this country was coming apart at the seams. We were in Southeast Asia . . . Good men were dying for America and for the Constitution. In the southern part of the United States we were marching for civil rights and Dr. King had been assassinated, and we lost the Kennedys. And to think that merely because I was a professional baseball player, I could ignore what was going on outside the walls of Busch Stadium . . . All of those rights that these great Americans were dying for, I didn't have in my own profession.

The more Flood mulled it over, the more certain he became that this was a risk he had to take. Twelve years earlier he had made a promise to himself that he would never accept being traded again. At the time, he was a two-year player with no credibility. Now he had an opportunity to effect a change for the good of all of the players. This was a righteous cause. Perhaps he would lose, but maybe he would do some good in the process. After all, the players who had challenged baseball in the past were not star centerfielders. No player as prominent as Flood had ever taken on baseball. His reputation alone would ensure that attention be paid to his cause. If he couldn't control the outcome, at least he could at least educate people about a system that he felt was morally corrupt.

In the third week of November, Flood called Miller and said that he was ready to sue baseball. The two men met for dinner in New York not long afterward. There were finances to discuss. Miller proposed that pending approval from the association's executive board, the union would pay all of Flood's legal bills as well as transportation for case-related activities.

Miller then told Flood that even if he won, he would not receive any financial damages. In the unlikely event that the court reversed itself, Miller explained, the only change that could be effected was for the future, not for what had already transpired.

Flood thought about this very carefully. Even if he wasn't to receive damages, he asked, wouldn't a victory be a boon to other players in the future?

Miller said it undeniably would.

Flood replied that that was good enough for him.

The executive board of the Players Association would be meeting in San Juan, Puerto Rico, in early December. Miller suggested that Flood attend and make his presentation to the board members in person. Flood agreed. Miller knew that if Flood was going to go through with this, he would need the association supporting him every step of the way.

Flood left for Puerto Rico from St. Louis. He stopped in Atlanta for a connecting flight, where he met with Tim McCarver, who was coming in from Memphis. McCarver was the new player representative for the Phillies. They rode together the rest of the way, and McCarver seized the opportunity to question Flood about what was driving him to pursue his course of action. The two had been teammates for close to ten years, and McCarver cared about Flood. He was concerned for him as a friend, and he also wanted Flood to join him on the Phillies; he valued Flood as a teammate and felt that he was still an effective player.

McCarver asked many of the same questions that Miller had already posed to him weeks earlier. He found Flood's sense of resolve admirable and was impressed by his principles, but he wondered what Flood was going to do for money.

Flood replied that certain things were more important than money.

McCarver had known Flood long enough to grasp that he wasn't kidding. While he may not have foreseen the impact that Flood's lawsuit would have, he knew that Flood had already thought things through and that, having committed himself, he was not about to turn back.

At the airport, the two players met Dal Maxvill, who, along with Joe Torre, represented the Cardinals on the executive board. Maxvill reportedly asked Flood, "Do you know that you're going to be out there like the Lone Ranger?" Flood nodded his head. For all the camaraderie in a major league clubhouse, Flood was essentially going at this alone.

The meeting of the executive board in Puerto Pico was significant because it was the first time that the players decided to meet in a city different from where the owners were conducting their winter meetings. The executive board consisted of twenty-seven men, including Miller and Moss. Moe Drabowsky, the man against whom Flood hit his first major league home run, was there as the representative for the Kansas City Royals. Reggie Jackson of the Oakland A's and Roberto Clemente of the Pittsburgh Pirates were the only representatives who weren't white.

In the late morning of December 13, Flood's issue was raised. Flood, who had been in his hotel room, was summoned to talk to the board. According to the minutes of the executive board meeting, later distributed by the association to its members, Flood said "that he felt there were great inequities to all the players in baseball's reserve system, and that he was no longer willing to be bought and sold as if he were a piece of property." After playing for so many years, he didn't believe that his career should be determined "exclusively by other persons." Flood said that since the owners were unwilling to consider any of the modifications to the reserve clause, he felt that something must be done to force their hand.

According to the notes, Flood stated that "shortly he would make public his position that he is entitled, as are other citizens, to receive offers from different employers, and that, if necessary, he planned to take legal action to obtain this basic right. He indicated that it was his intention to go through with his plans regardless of whether the Association gave its formal support, even though he recognized that the Association's assistance be of great help in securing a satisfactory result."

The board questioned Flood extensively, wanting to know his true intentions. They had to think about their constituents, and while they could empathize with Flood's predicament, there were bound to be some players who did not support him. The representatives were in a delicate situation. Like Miller, they didn't want Flood's case to damage the union, so, like Miller before them, they grilled him. He answered them in a steady, sober manner, making the same assurances to them that he'd made to Miller.

Tom Haller, the Dodgers' representative, asked what many on the board might have been thinking: Was Flood doing this because he was black? Was this a matter of race? Flood acknowledged that being black made him especially sensitive to the inequalities of the current system. He admitted that he had become increasingly aware of this during the past several years as black consciousness influenced African Americans across the country. But he made it clear that his action was not motivated by race. He was acting as a ball player for the benefit of other players, for whom he was prepared to risk his career.

The representatives considered the matter at length. The owners, they recognized, had refused to seriously negotiate modifications to the reserve clause. In reality the players felt that they had two options if they wanted to change their status: strike or go to court. In Flood, they had a man willing to take this fight on his own shoulders. The board voted 25-0 to support him. It was a crucial step in Flood's crusade.

*   *   *

After the meetings concluded, Miller contacted Arthur Goldberg. Goldberg was one of the most renowned lawyers in the country, and Miller had worked under him when Goldberg served as the general counsel to the Steelworkers' Union. In 1961, President Kennedy had appointed Goldberg to be Secretary of Labor; less than two years later, he nominated him to the Supreme Court. Goldberg was a Supreme Court Justice until he reluctantly accepted President Johnson's appointment to serve as the United States Ambassador to the United Nations. But Goldberg, who was against the war in Vietnam, was frustrated as ambassador and stepped down in the spring of 1968, returning to private practice.

Goldberg had written the majority decision on several antitrust cases while he served on the Supreme Court, and Miller considered him an expert. While he had some personal reservations about Goldberg, who he felt was self-centered, Miller nevertheless believed he would be an ideal choice to represent Flood. The fact that Goldberg had a national reputation could only lend prestige and publicity to the case.

When Miller and Moss had breakfast with Goldberg, Miller was amazed at how much Goldberg knew about the reserve clause. Goldberg was fascinated that something like it existed in American society—to him, as to Flood, it was in many ways so un-American. He admired Flood's courage in wanting to fight and was receptive to the pitch Miller and Moss made to him. Miller, though, was worried about something he had seen in the *New York Times* that very morning. Some members of the Democratic Party were interested in nominating Goldberg to run for governor of New York in 1970. Miller hoped a suit would make it all the way to the Supreme Court, but he didn't know how long that would take. It was hard for Miller to image the governor of New York

State arguing a case before the Supreme Court, so he asked Goldberg if he was serious about running for office. Goldberg assured him that he had no interest in being governor. He decided to take Flood's case.

Miller and Moss briefed Goldberg on the history of baseball's exemption and labor relations. Jay Topkis, a partner at Goldberg's firm who had written an article on the reserve system while a law student at Yale, and Max Gitter, an associate, would assist Goldberg in his work. On December 15, Flood, accompanied by Miller and Moss, was in New York to meet his lawyers. Flood was daunted at first, awed that he was being represented by such a powerful man, but Goldberg put him at ease. He talked about the case with confidence, knowledge, and conviction. Flood left the meeting feeling that he could not have been more fortunate.

The men began drafting a letter for Flood to send to the commissioner, which he did the day before Christmas. It read:

Dear Mr. Kuhn,

After 12 years in the major leagues, I do not feel that I am a piece of property to be bought and sold irrespective of my wishes. I believe that any system that produces that result violates my basic rights as a citizen and is inconsistent with the laws of the United States and [of] several states.

It is my desire to play baseball in 1970 and I am capable of playing. I have received a contract from the Philadelphia club, but I believe I have the right to consider offers from other clubs before making any decisions. I, therefore, request that make known to all the major league clubs my feeling in this matter, and advise them of my availability for the 1970 season.

Curt Flood

Kuhn's office was closed for the holidays, but before the year was out, he sent Flood the following response:

Dear Curt:

This will acknowledge your letter of December 24, 1969, which I found on returning to my office yesterday.

I certainly agree with you that you, as a human being, are not a piece of property to be bought and sold. This is fundamental in our society and I think obvious. However, I cannot see its applicability to the situation at hand. You have entered into a current playing contract with the St. Louis club which has the same assignment provision as those in your annual major league contracts since 1956. Your present contract has been assigned in accordance with its provisions by the St. Louis club to the Philadelphia club. The provisions of the playing contract have been negotiated over the years between the clubs and the players, most recently when the present Basic Agreement was negotiated two years ago between the clubs and the Players Association.

If you have any specific objection to the propriety of the assignment, I would appreciate your specifying the objection. Under the circumstances, and pending any further information from you, I do not see what action I can take and cannot comply with the request contained in the second paragraph of your letter.

I am pleased to see your statement that you desire to play baseball in 1970. I take it this puts to rest any thought, as reported earlier in the press, that you were considering retirement.

Sincerely Yours,
Bowie Kuhn

On one level, of course, Kuhn was correct: Flood *was* under contract. However, this was so only because of the reserve clause, which was at the very heart of Flood's unrest. Had he had the right to free agency when his contract expired, he might never have re-signed with Cardinals during his 1968 contract dispute.

Later that day, Flood publicly announced his intentions to sue baseball. He addressed the media, speaking with "consid-

Flood and Marvin Miller, the executive director of the Players Association, chat behind the scenes at ABC–TV studios in New York during an appearance on Howard Cosell's program. (Source: *Associated Press*)

erable emotion about his feelings," according to the *New York Times*. On January 3, Flood and Miller appeared on ABC–TV, interviewed by Howard Cosell, the most controversial broadcaster of his time. Cosell himself had been a lawyer and, as a Jew who had experienced discrimination in the television industry, was particularly sensitive to the issue of injustice and civil rights. Moreover, he wasn't afraid to express his indignation about what he felt was wrong.

Cosell pointed out that Flood was making $90,000 a year, which, he said, "isn't exactly slave wages." To that, Flood responded, "A well-paid slave is nonetheless a slave."

In another television interview, Flood told a reporter, "What I really want out of this thing is to give every ballplayer the chance to be a human being. And to take advantage of the fact that we live in a free and democratic society." Flood described the owner-player dynamic as a "master and slave relationship. As long as you do what I say [to] do, you're fine, that's great. As long as I can control you and keep you under my thumb."

Flood was not the first black athlete to make the slave analogy. Harry Edwards used it repeatedly, and Muhammad Ali would employ it as well. Though Flood was fighting for the rights of all players, this terminology brought the complicated and volatile issue of race to the forefront of his case. There were many white sportswriters and fans who regarded this kind of analogy as the ultimate sign of disrespect. Part of baseball's powerful myth was that players, especially minority players, should be grateful for what the game had done for them and ignore all that those players had done for the game.

Flood didn't believe that the players owed the game anything. If anything, it owed them the basic rights that a plumber or a sanitation worker or any other laborer would have. Of course, Flood made more than any garbage man (whose salary in 1970 would have been about a tenth of Flood's), and there was swift backlash against his complaints. He was ridiculed as a $90,000 slave. Dick Young, the most influential sportswriter in the country, chided Flood, and Bob Broeg, who had covered Flood for years in the St. Louis Post-Dispatch, wrote, "It is difficult indeed to be sympathetic to the little man, particularly when it really is not a matter of principle, but of principal." Again, a common response to Flood's suit was one of disbelief. How could a man so well paid be complaining about his civil rights?

Flood alienated and angered some fans and members of the press, but he also received some strong support. Many black journalists hailed Flood's struggle, and white columnists like Jim Murray, Red Smith, Shirley Povich, and Robert Lipsyte all sympathized with his platform. Putting a different slant on a similar theme, Larry Merchant wrote an article called "A Matter of Principle" for the *New York Post*, in which he argued that the fact that Flood was black gave him the necessary perspective to recognize the unfairness of the reserve clause. (As the author David Halberstam said in an ESPN interview years later, for a black player the reserve system "was a reminder of what had been done to their grandparents and great grandparents.") And Milton Gross, also of the *New York Post*, wrote that "what Flood is doing is not only suing for himself, but for the free agent kid, the rookie, the fringe player, the star and the super-star."

Still, it was hard for numerous fans, black and white, to understand Flood's position. Most of them would give their firstborn child to be able to play centerfield professionally, let alone make $90,000 a year doing it. Buddy Gilbert, Flood's teammate in the minor leagues, had long since retired. He was shocked when he read the news that Flood was suing baseball. He found Flood's number and called him to ask if he'd gone crazy. "For $90,000 a year, they can call me a slave all they want," he said.

On Friday, January 16, 1970, Flood formally filed suit, charging baseball with violating antitrust laws and the thirteenth amendment to the U.S. Constitution, which prohibited involuntary servitude. A hearing was set to consider Flood's request for immediate release from the reserve clause. The following day, the two league presidents, Joe Cronin of the American League and Chubb Feeney of the National League, issued a statement that reiterated that the reserve clause was "absolutely necessary" to baseball. Without it, they wrote, "professional baseball would simply cease to exist." Paul Richards, the general manager of the Atlanta Braves, went so far as to say that if the players got rid of the reserve clause "it would be like the Pope burning down the Vatican."

Criticism began to mount. John Quinn felt that Miller had

An editorial cartoon from the St. Louis Post-Dispatch that unfairly depicts Flood as a selfish player whose lawsuit only served to benefit him financially. (Source: *St. Louis Post-Dispatch*)

put Flood up to taking baseball to court. He remembered Flood's casual remark to the woman who approached them in New York back in December and was sure that Flood was Miller's dupe. Robin Roberts, now retired, said publicly that he didn't believe that it was Miller's idea, but that Flood was nevertheless doing the wrong thing. "I know Curt was upset over being traded by the Cardinals after twelve years, and the Cardinals handled it terribly," he said. "And the reserve clause *has* to be rewritten. But going to court is the wrong way."

Several prominent players were frustrated that all of the players weren't allowed to vote on whether the association should back Flood. Perhaps not surprisingly, some of the league's best-paid stars did not support Flood's action. No player was more adamant than Carl Yastrzemski, who said, "I think it could ruin the game." Yastrzemski, who was close with Red Sox owner Tom Yawkey and one of the highest paid players in baseball, added, "I'm for the Players Association. I think it has done a wonderful job in most respects . . . but we can't be constantly taking. We have to give something once in a while. We need the owners. It would hurt all of us tremendously if we created a gap between the players and the owners which couldn't be repaired."

Other players like Brock, Dick Allen, and Mets player representative Ed Kranepool came out in support of Flood. "Curt Flood's doing a marvelous thing for baseball, and many people don't know it," Allen said. "I don't have the intelligence to do what he's doing, but my hat's off to him."

Intelligence wasn't the only issue. In an interview with ESPN years later, Bob Gibson said, "I told him I'd be with him one hundred percent, but I'd be back a few hundred paces, just in case some of the fallout would hit him. I didn't want it to hit me too."

The pressure on Flood was severe. He was not a media darling like Ali or an intimidating presence like Bill Russell, and he was now facing a level of public scrutiny that was unlike anything he'd ever encountered on the playing field. Flood received various letters, the overwhelming majority of which were supportive. However it was the small quantity of hate mail that stuck with him, causing him to lose sleep. He was going to destroy the national pastime, they said. One stated, "Once you were compared with Willie Mays. Now you will be compared with Benedict Arnold."

In early February, Flood and his lawyers were in District Court in New York before Judge Irving Ben Cooper. They were seeking an injunction that would declare Flood a free agent so he could play in 1970. Kuhn and baseball's lawyers never forbade Flood from playing in 1970, but Goldberg knew that without permission from the court, Flood would have to remain out of the game in order to prove that he'd suffered damages. Without that, the case could have been dismissed or considered moot by the Supreme Court.

"Flood's case," Goldberg said, "is not designed to cripple or harass baseball. He desires to be treated as a free man. As for slavery," he continued, "the ancient Romans had high-priced slaves, some with access to the king's treasury—but they were still slaves. The basic concepts here are the morality and legality of the situation."

Goldberg contended that the previous Supreme Court decisions "do not apply now because times have changed." He pointed out the various industries that had to comply with antitrust laws. "They seem to be doing all right," he said.

Judge Cooper was a flamboyant character. Though he'd lived in the United States most of his life, he spoke with a pronounced English accent. Cooper enjoyed the high-profile nature of the case and used baseball jargon several times that afternoon. He called a "seventh inning stretch" after Goldberg's opening presentation, and when both sides had spoken, he said, "Now you have thrown the ball to me and I hope I don't muff it."

A month passed before Cooper made his decision. During that time, Flood was introduced to Herbert Alexander of Trident Press, who agreed to publish Flood's autobiography, which would be co-authored by Richard Carter, a black writer almost twenty years Flood's senior. Carter arrived in St. Louis at the end of February, shortly after Flood's thirty-second birthday, and they began to work—though in truth they did more drinking than they did writing.

On March 4, Judge Cooper denied Flood's request for an

injunction and stated that the case would have to go to trial. Neither side was surprised. Dick Young noted that even had Flood won the right to become a free agent, "I have the strangest hunch that every team in the majors suddenly would have found itself overstocked with centerfielders."

Following Judge Cooper's decision, Flood issued the following statement:

> The failure to obtain a restraining order means I've lost my one chance to play ball this year... I can only hope that after a full hearing on the merits that my position will be vindicated and that my career will not have been ended by the time lost pursuing what I believe to be right.

Reality was setting in. Flood's suit was not going to be resolved quickly. Meanwhile, his photography business, which had gone largely unattended, was now doing poorly, and he had not been able to concentrate on painting. His plan for the bar in Copenhagen fell apart. For the first time in his adult life, Flood was not in training camp. He was rudderless.

A few days later, Flood held a press conference at Zerman's office. He wore his biggest pair of sunglasses to hide the anguish on his face as he answered the same questions he had been answering for months. No, he wasn't trying to ruin the game. Yes, he was ready to resume playing at any time, though he knew his career was probably over.

"I don't think that one of the twenty-four [owners] in baseball will touch me with a ten-foot pole," he said. "In my own mind, I don't really expect to play again."

Flood said that there was no way he would sign with the Phillies, even though he'd been offered more than $100,000 to play for them. "I just will not sign that contract again," he proclaimed, meaning the one with the reserve clause in it.

By the end of March, Judge Cooper granted Flood's

motion for an early trial. Shortly before it began, Monte Irvin, a former Negro Leaguer and New York Giant who now worked in the commissioner's office, tried to contact Flood to try to arrange a sit-down meeting with Kuhn. Irvin informed Marion, who answered the phone in Flood's absence, that the commissioner was willing to work out a deal that would allow Flood to play for any National League team in 1970. Marion knew that if Flood played at all that season, his case would be considered moot. She told Irvin that the commissioner had no jurisdiction in federal court and wanted to know what he really wanted. Irvin said that the commissioner wanted everything to work out for everyone involved. He informed her that this was Flood's last chance. Marion thanked him and said goodbye.

Several days later, Kuhn sent Flood a telegram. It read: "I desired an opportunity to discuss with you personally your baseball career without prejudice to the basic issues involved in the pending litigation . . . If you reconsider I will continue to be available."

Flood did not bite. He and baseball were going to trial.

Meanwhile, Miller and Moss continued to negotiate the basic agreement with John Gaherin, the owners' representative. When all was said and done and the new agreement was signed, the players had gained increases in the minimum salary. More importantly, they had at last secured a provision for impartial arbitration. Although Kuhn was reluctant to relinquish any control, Gaherin knew that having an impartial arbitrator was a standard part of any labor contract. Sooner or later, the commissioner and the owners would have to accept this. Gaherin and Miller were able to placate Kuhn by allowing the commissioner to still have the final say in issues "that reflected the integrity of the game." All other issues—

disagreements regarding travel accommodations and club-house conditions—were to be decided by a third party appointed by the players and the owners. It may not have seemed groundbreaking at the time, but this provision would end up being one of the crucial factors in determining the future of the reserve clause.

After spending spring training visiting with each team, Miller returned to New York and accompanied Flood to court. Flood was represented by Goldberg and Topkis, while baseball was represented by four high-powered law firms. As it turned out, after months of coy deliberation, Goldberg had indeed accepted the Democratic nomination to run for governor, though his periodic absences did not have any adverse effects on Flood's case. He made the opening statements and did some questioning of witnesses, but it was Topkis, a distinguished courtroom presence, who would do the bulk of the work in court.

The main purpose of the trial for Flood was to establish, for the first time on record, the injustice of the reserve system—to expose it as a violation of antitrust laws and establish its detriment to the game's prosperity. The defense, in turn, was arguing that since the Supreme Court had already handed down two decisions on baseball's antitrust exemption, Flood's case was irrelevant. Furthermore, its position was that, without the reserve clause, baseball would be thrown into a "chaotic state." Baseball was a unique industry, it said, and the reserve system was essential to it.

Regardless of what transpired in the courtroom, the arguments would be most forcefully articulated in the post-trial briefs—thorough, heavily documented reports presented to the judge at the conclusion of the trial. In a case like Flood's, which dealt with the legalities of antitrust legislation as well as with legal precedent, the briefs were equally important to, if not more important than, the testimony from the trial itself. And no matter how Judge Cooper ruled, the losing party was sure to appeal.

The trial began on Tuesday, May 19, on the fifteenth floor of the Federal Courts Building in downtown Manhattan. Flood was the first to testify after the opening remarks. He was not in baseball shape and looked heavier around the face than he did while he was playing. Nevertheless, he was sharply dressed in a double-breasted, blue suit, and appeared as cool as ever. Inside, he was anything but. For months, he had been playing the role of articulate rebel in the press, but now, sitting in a courtroom, he was awestruck and nervous. When asked a question, Judge Cooper instructed condescendingly, Flood was to give a literal, straightforward answer. He was not to assume what others might have been thinking when recounting a conversation; he was being asked only to give the facts as he remembered them. If he didn't recall something, he was to say so and nothing more.

While Flood's lawyers had no doubt rehearsed him in the finer points of testifying, the difference between practice and the real thing was like the difference between taking batting practice and facing Bob Gibson in an actual game. Flood was flustered and he mumbled; both Judge Cooper and Goldberg repeatedly had to ask him to speak up. Early in his testimony, while he was trying to get his bearings, Judge Cooper asked, "Mr. Flood, I presume you are not finding this easy as getting up at bat, is that right?"

Flood conceded that he was not.

Goldberg focused on Flood's history of salary negotiations. Flood's earnings for each year in the majors were admitted as evidence and would subsequently be made public in the newspapers the following day. Though fans at the time were familiar with what the handful of top players earned, they were just

A cool customer, Flood poses for photographers on the steps of the Federal District Court in New York City. While he struck a brave posture for the cameras, Flood was riddled with anxiety during this time. (Source: *Associated Press*)

beginning to see—and resent—the disparity between their wages and those of a player like Flood, who didn't even hit many home runs.

While being cross-examined by the defense, Flood made a minor contradiction when he told defense attorney Mark Hughes that he wanted to abolish the reserve system completely; all along he had claimed that he merely wanted to modify it. While Flood's slip was simply a sign of nervousness, Hughes pounced on the inconsistency. Minutes later, he asked Flood what he thought would happen if every player were a free agent at the end of each season.

Goldberg quickly objected to the question, but Cooper allowed it.

Flood answered, "I think then every ballplayer would have a chance to really negotiate a contract just like in any other business."

Flood had recovered nicely. After all, the reserve clause in essence would have to be eliminated before it could be modified anyway.

Judge Cooper asked if Goldberg wanted Flood's answer stricken from the record.

"No, I like that answer," Goldberg replied.

The rest of the cross-examination was uneventful, and when Hughes was finished, Flood was undoubtedly relieved.

In a sense, Flood became almost secondary after his time on the witness stand. While he was the catalyst for the case, the lawsuit was more about baseball's exemption than it was about Curt Flood. Other than his testimony, the most memorable moment of the trial came two days later when Jackie Robinson testified. For black ballplayers, there was no greater icon, and Flood was overcome with emotion, humbled that the ultimate baseball pioneer had come out to advocate for him. A reverential silence fell over the courtroom as the gray-haired Hall of Famer, who would pass away two and a half years later, slowly walked to the witness stand.

Though physically diminished, Robinson was still mentally sharp and vibrant. Goldberg asked him what kind of changes could be made to the reserve clause that would benefit both the players and the owners. Robinson said, "I think the reserve clause is a one-sided thing in favor of the owners, and I think it certainly should at least be modified to give a player an opportunity to have some control over his destiny. Whenever you have one-sided systems, in my view, it leads to serious, serious problems, and I think that unless there is a change in the reserve clause that it is going to lead to a serious strike [by] ballplayers."

Robinson then spoke of Flood directly: "It takes a tremendous amount of courage for any individual—and that's why I admire Mr. Flood so much for what he is doing—to stand up against something that is appalling to him" For Flood, such words from this man must have been uplifting, to say the least.

Hank Greenberg testified next. He had been a great slugger for the Tigers in the 1930s, and after a successful career had gone into management, first as general manager of the Indians, and then as co-owner of the White Sox. He understood labor negotiations from both sides of the equation, and also knew how much of a gap existed between the players and the owners.

Greenberg was to the point. "I feel that the reserve clause is obsolete and antiquated," he said. "I see no reason why baseball shouldn't be able to function and even function better without the present contract as it exists today with a reserve clause."

Greenberg wasn't the only person with managerial experience who thought that baseball would survive a change to its system. Bill Veeck, a charismatic man who at different times had owned the Cleveland Indians, the St. Louis Browns, and the Chicago White Sox, thought that while a sudden elimination of the reserve system would be chaotic, a gradual elimination would not. Though Greenberg and Veeck (who was not currently running a team) were hardly representative of management's sensibilities, their testimony helped give credence to the notion that baseball could prosper under a new system.

Three more days of testimony followed before the Flood's team rested its case. It was hardly high drama. Most of the two thousand pages of testimony, produced in fifteen sessions, was filled with esoteric technical discussions. There were no star-tling surprises or declarations. There was no imploring of a jury. After Robinson's testimony, Flood found it difficult to stay focused.

Next came six days of Major League Baseball's witnesses, each asserting that "the game as we know it" would be destroyed if the reserve system were altered or eliminated. Without it, they claimed, rich clubs would simply dominate poor ones. Both Gene Ward in the *Daily News* and Leonard Koppett in the *New York Times* criticized the owners' notion of preserving "the game as we know it." What did that mean exactly? In recent years, teams had been added, others relo-cated; the pitching mound had been lowered, a new playoff format introduced. The game changed when it suited the owners; in this case, it was the reserve system that suited them.

Joe Garagiola was the lone ex-ballplayer to testify for the owners. "To me, this is the best system so far and I haven't heard anyone come up with a better one," he said. A surpris-ing number of players, past and present, ageed. They had never known anything but the reserve clause and perhaps feared that the owners were right: without it, baseball would be destroyed and with it their careers.

When the trial ended on June 10, both sides were given roughly one month to hand in their post-trial briefs to Cooper. A ruling was expected later in the summer. For Flood the experience had been grueling, but a case against the reserve clause was finally on record.

Some cynical sportswriters felt that Flood would win in the end by benefiting financially. "An out-of-court settlement will be reached," predicted Dick Young. "Flood will drop his suit and will play for the Phillies. As part of the settlement, he will be given all the back pay he now is missing."

But more progressive writers felt that serious strides had been made against an unjust system. "No matter what verdict is returned by Judge Cooper," Gene Ward wrote in the *Daily News*, "the owners will come up losers because the players ultimately will achieve a loosening of their bonds by strike or by the threat of strike, and there's nothing The Establishment can do to stop it." Articles by others, Red Smith and Robert Creamer among them, echoed this sentiment.

Yet in spite of the optimism expressed by some members of the media, Flood's spirits continued to sag. The 1970 season was almost half over, and he couldn't have felt farther from the game. He did work on his book with Carter but was still unable to paint. He continued to drink and his depression became more acute.

It had been a huge disappointment to Flood that not one major leaguer showed up to support him at the trial. Naturally, there would have been problems in attending. For one thing, it would have been risky for role players, who were more susceptible to demotions or trades. And players couldn't just leave their teams and fly to New York during the middle of the season without facing repercussions. Still, during the trial, the Yankees played four series in New York, while the Mets hosted three (including one against the Cardinals), and no one came. Flood was left wondering whether a greater showing of solidarity would have helped his cause.

No matter how much some players privately supported Flood, a public gesture of support was something that they were not comfortable with, as Bob Gibson explained on ESPN many years after the trial: "The reason nobody backed Curt up is because he was more or less expelled, blackballed from baseball, and it would have happened to anybody else too."

Dal Maxvill added: "I still had a few more years that I wanted to play without having the ownership of baseball not be happy with me, so I probably wouldn't have enough courage to do that." And in a 1997 interview with Spike Lee, Lou Brock said that the Cardinals' players were behind Flood but were uncertain of how to show their support. "He was a pioneer going forward on uncharted territory. And so everybody took a position: we'd stay and watch and see what happened."

Miller would later take responsibility for not encouraging the players to stick up for Flood. But at the time, not all of the players were one hundred percent behind the association. Their resolve had not yet been tested by a strike. Some still thought of the owners as benevolent patrons who had their best interests at heart. However, one thing Miller knew for certain was that the owners would not act unless they were forced to. Milton Gross of *The Post* agreed, noting that four major law firms represented the owners: "When you expend that kind of dough," he wrote, "chances are that you will battle to the bitter end before giving ground."

A ruling from Judge Cooper wasn't expected for months. In the meantime, Flood was aimless, keeping late hours and carrying on with women instead of working. In the beginning of August, Marion confronted him with a harsh reality: his photography business was about to go under. Flood did not want to deal with this, but his savings were drying up, and he had become delinquent in his alimony payments. After some investigation, Flood discovered that there was nothing he could do to resuscitate his finances. At a loss, he decided to leave the country rather than face the public embarrassment of his failing business ventures. While Marion may have been distressed by his choice of action, she was relieved that after months of paralysis, Flood was at least doing something. The two said their short-term goodbyes, and Marion returned to California while Flood went to Copenhagen.

Once he was in Denmark, Flood took a room in a little town called Vaethbeck, fifteen miles north of Copenhagen, that looked over a yacht basin. He began to paint again and resumed his plan to open a bar. He learned by mail—and subsequently read in the newspapers—that on August 12, Judge Cooper ruled against him, upholding the two previous Supreme Court decisions. Flood was not surprised. He was just one man fighting an uphill battle against an entire industry. What's more, he felt that race had played a part in the outcome. In his mind, there was no way that the court was going to let a black man win this case.

Miller had expected Cooper to rule in favor of baseball, in spite of recent court rulings that boxing and football were not exempt from antitrust laws. In a forty-seven-page opinion, Cooper wrote, "For the first time in almost 50 years opponents and proponents of the baseball reserve system have had to make their case on the merits and support it with proof in a court of law." But while he didn't feel that it was his place to determine the "fairness or reasonableness" of the reserve system, he did encourage both sides to consider negotiating modifications. Meanwhile, Flood's lawyers filed an appeal with the court of appeals, the second step in taking the case all the way to the Supreme Court.

As fall began, it became clear that Flood's legal troubles were worse than he had thought. The failed businesses now resulted in several lawsuits. Suddenly, being a reclusive expatriate looked damning. Even Flood recognized the contradictions of his current situation. On one hand, he was involved in a major lawsuit over baseball's economics; on the other, he was in small claims court as a result of his business ineptitude.

It was around this time that Flood got word that the Washington Senators had acquired the rights to negotiate with him. According to *Kiss It Goodbye,* Shelby Whitfield's book about that team, Senators' owner Bob Short came up with the idea at an owners' meeting the previous spring. When the commissioner announced to the owners that they would have to collectively pay the legal fees in the Flood case, Short suggested that since the Phillies couldn't sign him, they should be responsible for paying any lawyers. After the meeting, John Quinn scoffed at Short: Did he think that *he* could sign Flood? Short thought he could and ever since had been determined to bring Flood to the Senators.

Flood returned to New York and met with Short, Miller, Goldberg—who was in the middle of the gubernatorial election—and Max Gitter. The main concern was whether Flood would be jeopardizing his suit if he returned to the game. Goldberg concluded that since he had already missed one year, Flood had suffered damages and hence his case would not be compromised if he came back. In a series of meetings, Flood's lawyers proposed a contract that would grant him a no-trade clause, pay his entire salary upfront, and release Flood unconditionally if he and the Senators failed to come to terms on a contract the following year. On top of that, they wanted a guarantee from the owners that his playing again would not affect his suit.

Short had no problem with their proposal, but while Kuhn was willing to grant their last request—that should Flood play again, it would not affect his suit—the rest of it was entirely unacceptable to him. Short's involvement probably didn't help: he had never endeared himself to anyone in the baseball community. During the 1970 season, claiming that the Senators, long a losing organization, were virtually bankrupt, he threatened to move them out of Washington, D.C. He had also just traded for Denny McLain, who had been suspended for a portion of the season for gambling. Along with

A weathered, heavier Flood looks out from the Washington Senators' front office before his return to baseball in 1971. His comeback would be short-lived. (Source: *Sports Illustrated*)

Flood, he was a former star who was now more controversial than promising. That Short pursued both players during October distracted attention from the World Series, vexing Kuhn and the other owners.

There would be no special concessions made for either Flood or Short. If Flood wanted to play, he would have to sign the same contract that every other player signed. At first Miller balked, but Short insisted that even if it wasn't in writing, Flood was going to get everything he had asked for. He wasn't going through all this trouble to trade Flood or otherwise make him unhappy. When it came time to discuss salary, Short suggested he pay Flood around $100,000. Goldberg countered with $110,000 and Short quickly accepted. He also told Flood that he would help him straighten out some of his financial problems.

Flood was worried about how his return would be perceived. Some fans and players and certainly the press would think he was selling out, and Flood had to admit that it did not look good. However, he was desperate. "I still think the reserve clause stinks," he told the sportswriter Maury Allen, "[But] I'm paying alimony and I got five kids to support. That's enough to drive any man back into the game."

On November 4, Flood signed a one-year deal with the Senators and flew to Washington, D.C. to attend a press conference. Ted Williams, the great Red Sox outfielder, was now the Senators' manager. Williams had been critical of Flood's suit earlier in the year but now welcomed him to the team. After the conference, Flood went to Florida to play a few games in the Florida Instructional League and work his way back into shape. At the same time, he was being hounded for interviews by the media. In one, the *Associated Press* asked if he felt that his suit against baseball and everything he had been through had been worth it.

"I think so," Flood replied. "If I had to do it over again, I would. It brought a lot of attention for not only the public, but the ballplayers that are saddled with similar problems. We are not lawyers and our player contracts are not easy documents for the layman to read. If a man can get more money with normal bargaining rights, that's what it's all about."

Flood said that he didn't consider himself a martyr, and, when asked if he was coming back because he loved the game or because he needed the money, he said, "It's a combination of the two. I work and I do it for the money. I do not think I would play baseball if they didn't pay me." He added that playing baseball was the only way for him to earn the kind of money he had become accustomed to making. "I don't know how to do anything else," he said.

Of course, this wasn't entirely true. Flood had the intelligence and the talent to pursue other career paths, even if they were not as lucrative as baseball. But he was in a critical financial state and not in the proper frame of mind to think about his long-term future. He needed immediate relief. "Things are going so bad for me now," he joked to Maury Allen, "it would be just my luck to jump out of this window and live."

Flood's autobiography, *The Way It Is*, was released in the middle of February, less than a month after his thirty-third birthday. If Carter, Flood's ghostwriter, did not exactly capture Flood's voice in the book, he was at least able to convincingly recreate Flood's state of mind when they collaborated together. The book was more of an impressionistic collage of his life than a carefully documented history. It mentioned his playing experiences but didn't focus specifically on any one season. Flood's marriage and children were only briefly noted, though there was a loving tribute to the Jorgensens, as well as a moving description of Flood's relationship with his brother Carl.

The Way It Is also detailed the behind-the-scenes lifestyle of ballplayers: how they courted groupies, lived the lives of sex symbols, and used alcohol and amphetamines. But the crux of the book was a diatribe against the reserve system and the institutional racism in baseball. In all, it fiercely condemned much of baseball's public image as inaccurate and deceitful.

In reviewing the book, Bob Broeg noted that while Flood "comes across as a multi-talented man of many interests," he also "emerges as a cynic and as an unforgiving guy." And Dick Young blasted Flood for assorted factual errors, discounting the credibility of his arguments against baseball. "It is comical when a bright young man, who has proven himself a disaster in a couple of piddling business ventures, attempts to tell baseball how to run its finances."

But no matter its shortcomings, *The Way It Is* was a vivid and compelling representation of Flood's career in the big leagues, though not as sensational as *Ball Four*, Jim Bouton's infamous behind-the-scenes look at the game, released a year earlier. *The Way It Is* was more limited in scope but perhaps more illuminating about the ugly truths that existed in the game. In a glowing review in the *New York Times Book Review*, Jonathan Segal wrote, "Regardless of the outcome [of Flood's suit], Flood is the one who has done the struggling, made the demand and written an insightful book to explain his position."

Shortly after *The Way It Is* was published, Flood reported to spring training with the Senators. Almost immediately it was apparent that he was not right on the field. Technically, he was not hurt, but he was thirty-three and had been away from the game for a year and a half. Now he couldn't keep up with the younger, fitter ballplayers. At the plate he was overmatched, while in the field, his ability to judge fly balls was impaired for the first time in his life. At the same time, the pressure on him was intense. While other players never mentioned his suit, the fans wouldn't let him forget it. To many of them, he was a spoiled, self-righteous phony, and they let him have it.

In addition to the anxiety over his performance on the field and his finances off it, Flood had his lawsuit to deal with. The case had been argued before the court of appeals at the end of January, and it came as no surprise when, on April 7, the three-judge court upheld Judge Cooper's ruling. One of the judges, Judge Sterry R. Waterman, wrote:

> We freely acknowledge our belief that Federal Baseball was not one of Mr. Justice Holmes' happiest days, that the rationale of Toolson is extremely dubious and that, to use the Supreme Court's own adjectives, the distinction between baseball and other professional sports is "unrealistic," "inconsistent" and "illogical." [However] we continue to believe that the Supreme Court should retain the exclusive privilege of overruling its own decisions.

Though the court had gone so far as to question the reserve clause, it was another defeat for Flood. Now he and his lawyers would have to wait until the fall to learn if the Supreme Court would choose to hear the case. In the meantime, Flood grew surly with the media. Reporters constantly wanted to speak with him about his suit and his comeback. For the first time, he was not always amiable in return. The season started, and Flood was still not hitting. In his first twenty at-bats he had just three singles, two of them bunts. He was benched temporarily. Some of his teammates thought his difficulties were to be expected from someone who had been away from the game, but others saw something darker enveloping Flood. "Things are closing in on me," he told his teammate Mike Epstein one day while warming up before a game. During a trip to Yankee Stadium, Flood returned to the clubhouse to find a black wreath hung in his locker. He also received a letter that read, "Dear Nigger, You are a dead nigger." Flood was terrified that someone had found his way into the locker room to make these deliveries in person.

On April 27, Flood could no longer take it. After collecting seven hits—all singles—in thirteen games, he was through. He left the Senators, having already pocketed half of his year's pay (most of which went directly to his creditors), and went to the airport, where he sent Short a telegram. "I tried," he wrote. "A year and a half is too much. Very serious personal problems mounting every day. Thank you for confidence and understanding."

Short badly wanted to reach Flood before he left the country. "I'm sure that if I find Curt and talked to him, that I could persuade him to rejoin our ball club," he told the *Associated Press*. "It isn't the money. I'd just like to help Curt out." Joe Reichler, the former sportswriter who broke the St. Petersburg

Yacht Club story back in 1960, now worked in the commissioner's office. He rushed to Kennedy Airport to try to stop
Flood from leaving. Flood listened to him but could not be
stopped. He boarded a plane for Spain.

"I don't think we'll ever see him back in this country," a
member of the Senators' front office told Dick Young.
"Troubles like he has just don't go away."

In the early seventies, almost thirty-five hundred cases were
filed annually with the Supreme Court, with the court agreeing to hear less than two hundred of them. It is all the more
remarkable, therefore, that in the fall of 1971, the court
decided to hear Flood's case. Flood's suit had reached the
court in two years, which was unusually fast. Its high profile
and the intense media coverage no doubt helped to move it
along. Now both sides would file briefs and the case would
be argued in the spring of 1972.

All of a sudden, Flood's legal team thought it had a real
chance to win. Goldberg, who had been resoundingly
defeated in the 1970 New York gubernatorial election, and his
colleague Dan Levitt, an attorney who had clerked on the
Supreme Court for Goldberg in 1965 and for Justice Abe
Fortas from 1965 through 1967, were both intimately familiar
with the court and the kind of cases it accepted. It seemed
entirely reasonable to them that the justices were inclined to
overturn *Federal Baseball*; if they were going to adhere to
precedent, they had no reason to hear the case in the first
place. Under Goldberg's guidance, Levitt wrote the briefs,
wrapping his argument around Waterman's opinion. He felt
that the court of appeals had essentially said that while it
couldn't overrule an existing Supreme Court decision, the
Supreme Court itself might well change its views if it looked
at the decision again.

Oral arguments were heard before the court on March 20, 1972, by which point all nine justices had read the written briefs and their clerks had written memos on the case for them to examine. That morning, Goldberg and Levitt had breakfast together at the Hay-Adams Hotel, across the street from the White House. Goldberg told Levitt that his approach would be simple. He would make a short and direct statement, invite questions, and then sit down. This, he said, would be more effective than needlessly using up all of the thirty minutes allotted. The strategy struck Levitt as shrewd. Most lawyers wouldn't have the guts to do that, he thought.

This was Goldberg's first trip back to the Supreme Court since he had been a justice himself. He was a close friend to a number of the judges, particularly Justice William Brennan, though President Nixon had appointed four conservative judges since he left the court; one of them, William Rehnquist, had joined the bench in January, after the case had been selected to be heard. Goldberg should have felt at home; instead he was inexplicably rattled by his surroundings and, in spite of the strategy he had outlined to Levitt, launched into an unfocused, rambling presentation. The justices asked him questions along the way, as is customary, but several times they also urged him to move things along. Goldberg spent such a long time setting up the facts of the case that he suddenly found himself rushing. In the end, he used up all of his time to almost no purpose. He had done exactly the opposite of what he said he was going to do.

On the other hand, Lou Hoynes spoke for the defense and offered a coherent and succinct presentation. Yet, despite this contrast, Flood's legal team was not completely discouraged. Nothing the justices said during the argument indicated that they were hostile toward Flood's side. Goldberg had floundered, and from a rhetorical point of view his performance had been a flop, but there was nothing substantive in his presentation that created any problem. In general, while an extraordinary oral argument could have a decisive effect on a case, the justices more typically made up their minds when they decided to take the case in the first place.

In the days following the presentations, Levitt ran into Victor Kramer from the Arnold Porter law firm, one of those representing baseball, who indicated that like Levitt, he believed that baseball was going to lose the case. On the other hand, he also suggested that bribery was afoot. Earlier that year, the Senators had moved to the Dallas area to become the Texas Rangers. Now, Kramer said, the leaders of baseball were spreading rumors around Washington that if the court decided in favor of baseball, the city would get its team back. It is not certain that such a bribe was ever actually made or that any of the Justices would have seriously taken it into consideration (though some of them were indeed known to be big baseball fans).

In the meantime, tensions between the owners and the Players Association had reached a boiling point. The pension plan that was signed in 1969 was scheduled to run out at the end of March. When the owners refused the association's modest proposal for increases, the players were left in a quandary. Since the impartial arbitrator had been agreed to in 1970, the Players Association had won several minor disputes, rankling the owners, who felt that the players were nitpicking. This was not the way the owners were accustomed to doing business. They wanted to put an end to Miller, Moss, and the union once and for all.

The owners met on March 22 and agreed that they would not budge on the pension. They wanted to see if the players would hold their ground or panic and give in. During the meeting, the owners decided not to discuss the matter with the media, but Gussie Busch, who was more incensed than ever by the players, couldn't keep his feelings to himself. He told reporters, "We voted unanimously to take a stand. We're not going to give them another goddamn cent. If they want to strike—let 'em."

Miller did not believe that the players really knew what it meant to strike. They weren't paid in winter, and didn't have the financial resources that the owners did to fall back on. Quietly, Moss and Miller prepared to give in. But once they met with the player representatives, everything changed. The players were infuriated with the owners' tactics and with Busch's rant, which they took to be representative of how the owners as a group felt about them. Their pride had been challenged, and now they wanted to go ahead with a strike. Miller, in his gentle way, talked them through their decision, reiterating that they would be hurt by a strike as well. But the players were adamant, and so it was agreed: as of March 31, they were on strike.

This was by far the greatest test that the Players Association had ever faced. The season was supposed to have begun; instead, there were no games at all. Fans were disillusioned; the newspapers were filled with outrage. The owners were floored. Yet the players hung together, practicing at high school fields and in local gyms. They were losing money, but the owners were losing even more. Additionally, the owners were not as unified as the players were. Some owners wanted to wait out the strike, while others realized that it wasn't practical to be losing so much money, especially over something as trifling as the pension fund.

Miller and Gaherin eventually reached a compromise, and the strike ended on April 13. Nearly two weeks of the season were missed, a total of eighty-six games. The fans and the media directed their criticism at the players, but in reality it was the owners who were the losers. The union had proved its mettle. The owners could not bully the players any longer. The union was growing stronger due in large part to the arrogance of the owners and to their lack of unity and vision.

Flood's suit concluded on June 19, 1972. According to *The Brethren*, Bob Woodward and Scott Armstrong's book about the Supreme Court, for some time the justices' votes were split four-four. (Justice Powell did not vote because he owned stock in Anheuser-Busch Inc. Even though he supported Flood, Powell regarded participating in the decision as a conflict of interests.) Finally, though, Chief Justice Burger switched his vote, and the Supreme Court upheld *Federal Baseball* by a vote of five to three. President Nixon's two other appointees, Justices Rehnquist and Blackmun, ruled against Flood. Justices Douglas, Marshall, and Brennan ruled in Flood's favor. Had the vote been cast several years earlier, when the leaning of the court was more liberal, the decision might have been different. Now Flood and would-be free agent baseball players were casualties of a more conservative judiciary.

Justice Blackmun wrote the long-winded and sentimental majority decision. The initial portions of a decision are meant to provide the factual background of the dispute, but Blackmun went to an extreme, listing factors that supported each side before coming to his ruling. He sited famous, romanticized works of baseball literature like "Casey at the Bat" and referred to eighty-seven great ballplayers from the past (with no African Americans among them until Justice Marshall objected, and the names Jackie Robinson, Roy Campanella, and Satchel Paige were added.) In reality, everybody reading Blackmun's self-indulgent opinion knew enough about the situation to require no introduction.

Blackmun's fascination with old ballplayers and "the game as we know it" revealed a nostalgic view of baseball—a view that probably doomed Flood's cause.

But though the case ended in defeat for Flood, the decision was filled with ambiguity and even hope. Blackmun conceded that "professional baseball is a business . . . engaged in interstate commerce" and that "with its reserve system enjoying exemption from the federal antitrust laws, baseball is, in a very distinct sense, an exception and an anomaly."

Blackmun added: "We continue to be loath, 50 years after *Federal Baseball* and almost two decades after *Toolson*, to overturn those cases judicially when Congress, by its positive inaction . . . has allowed those decisions to stand for so long."

In essence, the court was saying that *Federal Baseball* was wrong, but that the Justices were not going to overturn it. It passed the buck to Congress, implying that if the legislature wanted to take action against the reserve system, it was free to do so. Many sportswriters were outraged: "This is the equivalent of an umpire admitting that he blew one, but refusing to change his decision," wrote Larry Merchant in the *New York Post*. Shirley Povich agreed, writing that "the court put a weak defense of baseball's antitrust exemption, and then tossed the ball to Congress which has consistently refused to mess with any baseball legislation, pro or con."

The contradictory nature of the ruling was blatant. In his dissenting opinion, Justice Douglas pointed out that "Baseball is today big business that is packaged with beer, with broadcasting, and with other industries." But it was Justice Marshall who added the most direct condemnation of the reserve system:

Americans love baseball as they love all sports. Perhaps we become so enamored of athletics that we assume that they are foremost in the minds of legislators as well as fans. We must not forget, however, that there are only some 600 major league baseball players. Whatever muscle they might have been able to muster by combining forces with other athletes has been greatly impaired by the manner in which this Court has isolated them. It is this Court that has made them impotent, and this Court should correct its error.

Miller had all along suspected that it would be impossible to take down the reserve clause through antitrust litigation. Though Flood's case was strong, a great reluctance on the part of the courts to reverse a decision by the venerated Justice Holmes—along with their idealized notions of the national pastime—superceded baseball's clear similarities to other industries. As a result, baseball's exemption remained intact. The owners felt that they had finally won one.

But would their victory last? Leonard Koppett wrote in *The Sporting News*, "In the long run, the Flood case will prove to be a turning point in the battle against the reserve clause, not a defeat. It has already accomplished two enormous things for the players. It has been an educational process for players and public, spelling out the real issues and real alternatives, and it has forced the club owners to bargain on the reserve clause, an offer they rigidly resisted until the Flood case began."

Larry Merchant concurred, noting in the *New York Post* that "[w]hen the ballplayers finally do get a better deal, Curt Flood will have played a role in it. He struck out, but not before he fouled off so many pitches that he helped wear down the other side."

Merchant's analogy was particularly apt considering the kind of team-first player Flood had been. And Miller did sense that the case helped pave the way for more serious negotiations with the owners about the reserve clause. The players, as a whole, had benefited. Sadly, he realized, "Flood is probably the only real loser in this case."

Chapter Six
Aftermath
(1973–1997)

Flood was not surprised at the Supreme Court decision when he read about it in a newspaper several days later, but it was still a crushing disappointment. His pursuit of professional freedom had begun the morning that he was traded to the Phillies almost three years earlier. When it came to a conclusion, he was thousands of miles from where he had once been.

Opting for the warm climate of Spain over Denmark, Flood settled in Majorca, a port town. He already spoke Spanish from his time playing winter ball in Venezuela, and he married a woman named Ann, who had a teenage son. Flood ran a small pub called The Rustic Inn. One of his old bats and his mitt hung behind the bar. The town was a popular stop with U.S. Navy personnel, and Flood kept in touch with events back home by speaking with the sailors who came through town. Howard Cosell sent him recordings of recent boxing matches for Flood to play at the bar.

American reporters made sporadic attempts to track Flood down, but once his case left the headlines, people forgot about him soon enough, much to his relief. The turmoil his life had become had been too much for him. "My ulcer has healed," he told a *Sports Illustrated* reporter who did manage to reach him in the fall of 1973. "I smoke only one pack of cigarettes a day instead of three. I'm a whole person again, you dig? I got my wife, my boy, and my dog. I'm Mr. Anybody. That's what quitting baseball did for me."

Flood found comfort in relative anonymity, but he was not able to escape thoughts about his lawsuit. He felt that if he had had six hundred players behind him, the reserve clause would have been toppled. He continued to drink and after several years had troubles with the local Spanish authorities and abandoned his bar. Flood moved to another Spanish town, Andorra, where he worked as a carpet layer, then later lived in Puerto Rico and the Dominican Republic before coming back home to Oakland in 1976. When he returned, everything in the baseball world had changed.

Instead of looking to compromise with the players after the Supreme Court ruling, the owners dug in their heels, continuing to cling to the reserve clause. Miller, however, remained determined to end the reserve system. He had long argued that paragraph 10a of the player's uniform contract read that if a player and team could not agree to terms on a contract by March 15, the previous year's deal could be renewed for just one season—not, as the owners interpreted, in perpetuity. If a player played for a full season under the renewed, unsigned contract, Miller reasoned, at the end of that season he should be declared a free agent.

Ever since the Players Association had secured impartial arbitration as part of its basic agreement, Miller had been yearning to test his interpretation of paragraph 10a. On a few occasions in the early 1970s, he had almost had his chance: Several players—including Bobby Tolan, Sparky Lyle and

Ted Simmons—had been unable to come to terms with their teams on a new contract and had chosen instead to play out their option year without one. Had they finished out the season that way, they would have gone to arbitration. In each case, however, management presented a mutually agreeable contract before the season ended, which perhaps suggested that the owners were at least conscious of the wording of paragraph 10a and the vulnerability it presented.

Now, with Flood's trial over, Miller revisited the notion of overturning the reserve clause through arbitration. He explained this idea to the players. Flood's case had failed on the grand stage, but here was a nuts-and-bolts strategy that could really work. Finally, in 1975, Dodgers pitcher Andy Messersmith, a two-time twenty-game winner, could not come to terms with his team. The point of contention was that the Dodgers refused to give Messersmith a no-trade clause, a feature almost unheard of at the time. Messersmith decided to play out his option with the intentions of taking it to arbitration at the end of the season. Here was a prime opportunity to challenge paragraph 10a. Miller, though, wanted insurance in case Messersmith and the Dodgers agreed to a deal late in the season, so he enlisted the help of Dave McNally, a veteran pitcher. McNally had enjoyed a terrific career, but after sustaining an injury while playing for the Expos in spring training, he had returned home to Montana and was all but retired. McNally agreed to lend his name to the case even after the Expos owner made a surprise visit to McNally's home and offered him $25,000 just to show up to spring training the following year—no questions asked. It was another sign that the owners feared arbitration and what it meant for the reserve clause.

As it turned out, the Dodgers and Messersmith never worked out a contract, and at the end of the 1975 season, Peter

Seitz, an impartial arbitrator agreed on by both the owners and the Players Association, heard Messersmith and McNally's case. Seitz granted free agency to A's pitcher Catfish Hunter a year earlier because Oakland's owner Charlie Finley had not fulfilled a contractual obligation. Now the question in front of Seitz was how paragraph 10a should be interpreted. Seitz considered the matter at length and before issuing his decision urged the owners and the union to work on modifications of the reserve system—a familiar refrain. The owners declined. His efforts to initiate a compromise unsuccessful, Seitz ruled in favor of the players. The owners immediately fired Seitz and appealed the decision in the courts, but their efforts were in vain. The reserve system was finally dead.

The owners still stalled the next spring when negotiating the new basic agreement and even briefly locked the players out of spring training camps. At one point, Finley suggested that they should just make all of the players free agents but Miller was onto this stratagem: if every player was a free agent, the market would be depressed, which wouldn't benefit the players. Better to have a trickle of free agents every season, making it a sellers' market. Fortunately for the players, the other owners loathed Finley so much that they completely ignored his sly proposition.

In the end, the two sides agreed that after six years of service at the major league level, players would become free agents. The balance of power had shifted. The era of free agency had begun. It was the beginning of a new day, perhaps the most important thing to happen to the game since Jackie Robinson. But while it was the players' greatest victory, it was the low point of Flood's life.

Flood returned to Oakland a shattered man. The players had finally won their freedom, a freedom that he had contributed mightily to, sacrificing more than anyone in the process, but he did stand not to reap any of the rewards. When, after Seitz's decision, Richard Reeves, a writer for *Esquire* magazine, went looking for him to do a story, a friend of Flood cautioned, "Maybe you should leave him alone. He took on something very big and it broke him."

"He's like an exposed nerve," Richard Carter told Reeves.

When Reeves did contact him by phone, Flood begged him, "Please, please don't come out here. Don't bring it all up again. Please. Do you know what I've been through? Do you know what it means to go against the grain in this country? Your neighbors hate you. Do you know what it's like to be called the little black son of a bitch who tried to destroy baseball, the American Pastime?"

Of course, Flood had not destroyed baseball. In fact, after a wildly successful 1975 World Series and the advent of free agency, the sport was more popular and as profitable as ever. Reeves eventually met with Flood and tagged along to a function at which Flood spoke to some students. Also there as a reporter was Bill Madlock, a major league baseball player who worked for the local sports television station during the off-season. Madlock told Reeves that if it hadn't been for Flood, he wouldn't be living in a big house and getting paid handsomely to go to banquets during the winter. "He says he's doing fine," Madlock said. "That's not true, is it?"

It wasn't. Flood was far from fine. Several months later, he fractured his skull falling down a flight of stairs while drunk. Murray Chass, a reporter for the *New York Times*, went to visit him in the fall and observed a man who seemed "to be hiding from the outside world, a man prevented by his own pride from letting people know what his life is really like."

Flood looked smaller and more fragile than ever. He spoke quietly over drinks, puffing on cigarette after cigarette. "The things that I did, I did for me . . . because I thought they were right," he said. "But what I did then is [relevant] today only because it happens that other people have benefited by it and that's cool. The guys are making more money and deservedly so. They're the show. They're it. They're making money because they work hard."

Flood admitted that he was lost without the game. "When you do something for twenty years," he said, "that's all you really know."

In 1978, Flood's old friend Sam Bercovich bought the local radio rights from Charlie Finley to broadcast A's games. Bercovich got Flood a job as an announcer. It was ironic that Flood, the face of the struggle for players' rights, got a job for Finley, whose baseball career would not survive free agency. Perhaps it was Finley's way of getting under Commissioner Bowie Kuhn's skin: the two despised one another. What could it hurt if hiring Flood to do small-time radio irked Kuhn and the other owners?

But Flood was distracted and unfocused during the broadcasts. He was withdrawn and never got acclimated to the back-and-forth banter that makes for successful announcing. Flood would space out and have to be prompted to rejoin the conversation and the game.

Tom Boswell, a baseball writer for the *Washington Post*, saw Flood that year. He looked, Boswell recalled later, "like a shy, hypersensitive ghost of himself. Though only forty-one, he seemed far older. His wounds were deep. His sense of isolation was almost palpable." Flood was, as his former Senators teammate Mike Epstein described him, "a man who has been tied to the mast and has taken one lash too many."

If Flood was wounded, he was at least starting to garner appreciation from ballplayers. Many of the veterans who had been active during Flood's playing days approached him and thanked him for the road he had paved. "All today's baseball players should thank Curt Flood, who got the whole thing started," said Rod Carew, who in 1979 signed a five-year contract with the Angels worth about $4 million. Carew was just one of many players who cashed in after free agency was introduced.

For his part, Miller wasn't about to let Flood's sacrifice go unnoticed. Every spring, when he made the rounds to each team's spring training facility, his final words to his increasingly-wealthy unionists was the same: "Curt Flood got you these things."

Free agency in baseball was on some level inevitable. The owners were not going to be able to deny players their right to self-determination forever. Television had introduced big money into the game, the sort of revenue that had simply never existed before. By the time Messersmith and McNally went to arbitration, sportsmen-owners like Gussie Busch, who had entered the game out of a combination of competitiveness and vanity, were fast becoming dinosaurs. A new breed of owners like George Steinbrenner and Ted Turner was prepared to spend top dollar for talent. Turner, who owned the cable network WTBS, put the Atlanta Braves on prime-time television and proved that a team didn't even have to win to be profitable so long as it sold ample airtime to advertisers.

The owners' old fear that free agency would ruin the game was clearly invalid. After free agency began, baseball prospered. In spite of continued expansion, competitive balance improved—there have been fewer sustained dynasties and fewer hopeless long-term doormats since 1976 than ever before—which created broader geographical interest. Attendance boomed, and total revenue in the game leapt from about $75 million in 1964 to $3.5 billion in 2001—with players earning their fair share.

Some fans complained about the player mobility that accompanied free agency, but while it is easy to look back before free agency and regard players as loyal and virtuous, that loyalty was coerced, its perks benefiting only a handful of stars. Men like Willie Mays and Carl Yastrzemski profited nicely under the old system, but they did so at the expense of their lesser-known peers. Of course, free agency did change the relationship that fans and the press have with the players. In the 1950s and 1960s, players were viewed as the guys next door. Most of them had regular jobs in the off-season and lived in middle-class neighborhoods. With free agency, all that changed. Players were more like other entertainers now—rich, removed, elite. At the same time, it can be argued that free agency added a new component to baseball, creating an off-season intrigue that carries its own particular brand of excitement.

However free agency affected the relationship of fans to baseball, there is no disputing that the reserve system was patently wrong and that Curt Flood's fight to overturn it was both courageous and appropriate—and would have been even had it ruined the game as the owners swore it would. Flood took his stand so that players could have the rights that every other American worker at least in theory possesses. The Messersmith-McNally ruling officially broke the old system, but it was Flood who made the world stand up and take notice of baseball's exploitive structure.

Slowly but surely Flood moved on. By the early 1980s he had a job with the Little League for the Oakland Recreation Department. Some of his famous friends, like Reggie Jackson and Joe Morgan, contributed equipment for the league. If Flood was not back in Major League Baseball, he was at least back in the game in a tangible, therapeutic way. George

Powles had been one of his greatest teachers, and now Flood had the opportunity to help kids out in a similar capacity.

In the mid-eighties, Flood married for the third time to Judy Pace, a television actress. She had been a friend of Flood since the late sixties, and she proved to be a stabilizing influence. Flood stopped drinking and smoking, and he emerged from a decade-long stupor. By the late eighties he served as commissioner of the short-lived Senior League, a professional league for middle-aged players.

During this period, Flood was called on to participate on several panels held by the commissioner's office. Peter Ueberroth, a more sensitive commissioner than Kuhn had been, made attempts to examine the racial dynamics in the sport, particularly in the inner cities where baseball's popularity had waned.

Flood's actions were embraced in Oakland, but on a national level he was still largely neglected—even among African Americans. Flood had not been a black icon like Muhammad Ali, Jim Brown, or Bill Russell. Those men had an aura of danger about them. They were tough guys, famous for not taking any guff from anyone. Before his suit, Flood was hardly a household name, even in the black community. He was one of a number of stars in the league, but not nearly so visible as Willie Mays, Hank Aaron or Frank Robinson. Unless you knew him personally, he was the last guy the average fan expected to take such a controversial stand.

Furthermore, the black community may have had trouble relating to Flood because of the distance between its daily struggles and his moral argument. Flood's stand had been articulated through the complicated language of law. It was about a particular clause in the player's uniform contract, a technical argument that was not nearly as immediate as Muhammad Ali's refusal to serve in the army. Black people may have supported Flood in theory, but they never latched onto his case; they never really identified with his struggle.

Flood was honored by a number of civil rights organizations, yet he never felt properly acknowledged. Harry Edwards, a special advisor to Ueberroth during the late eighties, at one point said to Flood that it was important to remember that people had their own everyday battles to fight. "One of the things I have learned," Edwards said, "is that you always want to stand up for the black community, but never be disappointed when the black community is not standing with you."

Still, the resentment at being an underappreciated outcast did not dissipate for Flood immediately. He felt as if something was due him, and he could be dismissive of writers, especially white writers, who wanted him to recount his story yet again. Eventually, though, Flood began to accept the way in which the world at large incorporated his efforts. "People try to make a Greek tragedy out of my life and they can't do it," Flood said with a smile to Joan Ryan of the *San Francisco Chronicle* in 1995. "I have never felt I gave up too much. All the things I got from it, they're all intangibles. They're all inside me. Yes, I sacrificed a lot—the money, maybe even the Hall of Fame—and you weigh that against all the things that are really and truly important that are deep inside you, and I think I succeeded."

"I did it because I believed in the American dream," Flood told Ryan. "I believed that if you were right that nine smart men on the Supreme Court would say that."

Even though the Supreme Court hadn't supported Flood, in the final analysis he was vindicated. In spite of the labor disputes that continued to divide the players and the owners, the game had survived free agency and flourished—a fact that was conceded even by Gussie Busch in the 1990s at an old timers' game. The old man shook Flood's hand and told him Flood that he'd been right, and that he wished the owners had listened to him. "It would have saved us a lot of money," he said.

In 1994, Don Fehr, the executive director of the Players Association, invited Flood to a meeting of the player representatives. This was during the most devastating strike in the game's history, which ultimately led to the cancellation of the World Series. It was an emotional time for the players, and their spirits were lagging. When Flood was brought into the meeting in an Atlanta hotel room, the player representatives gave him a standing ovation that lasted several minutes. Flood spoke with the players and emphasized the need for unity, reminding them of everything that players had fought for and sacrificed in the past to get to the point where they were now. It was his last great moment in the game.

In the spring of 1996, Flood was diagnosed with throat cancer. By the end of the year he was admitted to the UCLA Medical Center with pneumonia. Surrounded by family and friends, he remained upbeat. He did not want his room to be filled with long faces and sorrow. He wanted it crackling with life.

Flood died on January 17, 1997, one day before his sixtieth birthday. The Reverend Jesse Jackson and the columnist George Will delivered the eulogies at his funeral. Bob Gibson, Bill White, Maury Wills, Joe Morgan, and Lou Brock were among the former ballplayers in attendance, along with Flood's children from his first marriage and Judy Pace and her children.

Gibson remembered the personal side of his old roommate. He told the *Los Angeles Times*, "Curt had a way of bringing you back to reality when you got a little too high. When you were down and out and didn't think anything could be funny, he could make you smile."

"He was a man who dared to live by the strength of his conviction," Maury Wills added. "Most of us were not courageous enough to take that stand, challenging the owners. I know I wasn't."

These were kind words indeed. Moreover, Joe Garagiola, the lone former ballplayer to testify against Flood, told *New York Times* columnist Murray Chass, "I thought if the reserve clause went, baseball was going. . . . I was so wrong I can't begin to tell you. It took a lot of guts for him to do what he did."

Upon Flood's death, a smattering of articles praising his courage and his contribution to the game appeared in newspapers across the country. Flood's sacrifice had gained currency among older journalists who used his stand and subsequent lack of recognition as a platform to criticize modern players as self-centered and materialistic—ironic, given how Flood was portrayed at the time of his trial. The Cardinals paid tribute to him as well, holding a pre-game ceremony in his honor in 1997. Judy Pace was on hand, and she threw out the first ball.

Flood was further recognized in 1998 when, encouraged by both the owners and the players, Congress passed the Curt Flood Act. The act removed baseball's exemption from antitrust laws as it pertained to players' right in labor relations, giving them the same rights other professional athletes had. But it did not address baseball's exemption in any other form. It did not deal with franchise relocation, the minor leagues, intellectual property, or the amateur draft. For all intents and purposes, the exemption was still intact. Marvin Miller knew anything agreed upon by both the players and the owners was to be regarded with extreme suspicion. It was a hollow gesture, he thought, an honor that did not do justice to Flood's legacy.

Ultimately, though, Flood's legacy is a complicated one. His lawsuit was too intricate to boil down to a neat, tidy sound bite, so impressions of his exact role in baseball history have been vague and often erroneous. Had Flood ultimately won his suit, he would be remembered more vividly as a pioneer. As Dick Young, one of Flood's most vehement critics, predicted in 1970, "If he wins, his case will be historic, and Curt Flood's fame will surpass anyone in Cooperstown. If he loses, well, when is the last time you heard of George Toolson?"

In losing, Flood missed his chance at becoming an enduring symbol of the civil rights movement, but upon close examination it is clear that, as with Rosa Parks, fame was never the goal. Flood did what he did because he thought it was right. Marvin Miller concluded about Flood, "When you find somebody like Flood who was not just a superb performer and great teammate, as all of his teammates from the St. Louis Cardinals will tell you, but someone who thought about social problems and about injustice and who was willing to sacrifice a great deal to try and change things, you have a genuine role model. I think the integrity of a man like that is so impressive that it's hard to describe."

Flood had flaws—as a father, a husband, a businessman, even as a ballplayer. However, he never gave up on his beliefs or his desire for improvement of himself and his surroundings. His life took a course that he never in his wildest dreams could have imagined as scrawny kid making trick catches on the ballfields of Oakland. He took a simple stand against baseball, based on simple principles of fairness and justice—principles he held on to when it would have been so much easier to let them go.

When Flood was a player, one could have said (and some people did): *Well, he's not as fast as Brock, he doesn't hit as well as Cepeda, and his arm is only so-so. But the thing about Flood is that he'll give you everything he has.*

It's natural to celebrate a man who does what he thinks is right against all odds when he ends up winning. But though

Flood lost his case, his decision to stand up for what he believed in isn't any less significant, its impact no less great. A victory can't always be judged by an initial verdict—or even a second or a third. Sometimes years, even decades have to pass before a person's actions can be assessed, his sacrifices recognized.

For Curt Flood, the real sacrifice would have been reporting to the Phillies after his trade without saying a word.

CURT FLOOD'S CAREER STATISTICS

Year	Ag	Tm	Lg	G	AB	R	H	2B	3B	HR	RBI	BB	SO	AVG	OBP	SLG
1956	18	CIN	NL	5	1	0	0	0	0	0	1	0	1			
1957	19	CIN	NL	3	3	2	1	0	0	1	1	0	0	.333	.333	1.333
1958	20	STL	NL	121	422	50	110	17	2	10	41	31	56	.261	.317	.382
1959	21	STL	NL	121	208	24	53	7	3	7	26	16	35	.255	.305	.418
1960	22	STL	NL	140	396	37	94	20	1	8	38	35	54	.237	.303	.354
1961	23	STL	NL	132	335	53	108	15	5	2	21	35	33	.322	.391	.415
1962	24	STL	NL	151	635	99	188	30	5	12	70	42	57	.296	.346	.416
1963	25	STL	NL	158	662	112	200	34	9	5	63	42	57	.302	.345	.403
1964	26	STL	NL	162	679	97	211	25	3	5	46	43	53	.311	.356	.378
1965	27	STL	NL	156	617	90	191	30	3	11	83	51	50	.310	.366	.421
1966	28	STL	NL	160	626	64	167	21	5	10	78	26	50	.267	.298	.364
1967	29	STL	NL	134	514	68	172	24	1	5	50	37	46	.335	.378	.414
1968	30	STL	NL	150	618	71	186	17	4	5	60	33	58	.301	.339	.366
1969	31	STL	NL	153	606	80	173	31	3	4	57	48	57	.285	.344	.366
1971	33	WSA	AL	13	35	4	7	0	0	0	2	5	2	.200	.300	.200
15 Seasons				1759	6357	851	1861	271	44	85	636	444	609	.293	.342	.389
162 Game Avg				162	585	78	171	25	4	8	59	41	56	.293	.342	.389
Career High				162	679	112	211	34	9	12	83	51	58	.335	.391	.421

Postseason Batting

Year	Round	Tm	Opp	G	AB	R	H	2B	3B	HR	RBI	BB	SO	AVG	OBP	SLG
1964	WS	STL	NYY	7	30	5	6	0	1	0	3	3	1	.200	.273	.267
1967	WS	STL	BOS	7	28	2	5	1	0	0	3	3	3	.179	.258	.214
1968	WS	STL	DET	7	28	4	8	1	0	0	2	2	2	.286	.333	.321
3 World Series				21	86	11	19	2	1	0	8	8	6	.221	.287	.267

Source: www.baseball-reference.com

AVERAGE SALARY OF MAJOR LEAGUE BASEBALL PLAYERS

Year	Average Salary	Top Salary	
1967	25,955	125,000	(Willie Mays)
1972	39,044	200,000	(Hank Aaron)
1976	110,024	640,000	(Catfish Hunter)
1980	248,570	1,125,000	(Nolan Ryan)
1985	473,496	2,130,300	(Mike Schmidt)
1990	483,399	3,200,000	(Robin Yount)
1995	962,323	9,237,500	(Cecil Fielder)
2000	1,921,939	15,714,286	(Kevin Brown)
2005	2,479,125	26,000,000	(Alex Rodriguez)

Source: SABR and the MLBPA

CHRONOLOGY

1938: Curt Flood is born in Houston, Texas.

1947: Jackie Robinson and Larry Doby break the color barrier in the National and American Leagues respectively.

1955: Flood signs a professional contract of $4,000 to play for the Cincinnati Reds; Rosa Parks refuses to give up her seat on a Birmingham bus, initiating the boycott of the Birmingham bus system.

1956: Flood plays minor league ball in South Carolina, then makes his major league debut in September with the Reds. He also plays winter ball in the Dominican Republic.

1957: Flood plays his second year of minor league ball, this time in Georgia. He is again called up to the Reds at the end of the season, and records his first big league hit, a home run against the Cubs. After the season, Flood and Joe Taylor are traded to the Cardinals in exchange for Willard Schmidt, Marty Kutyna and Ted Wieand.

1959: Flood marries Beverly Collins.

1960: Lunch counter sit-ins across the country launch the civil rights movement.

1961: Johnny Keane takes over as Cardinals manager midway through the season.

1962: The Cardinals integrate their spring training living facilities in St. Petersburg, Florida; Flood meets John and Marion Jorgensen.

1963: Flood collects 200 hits and wins the first of seven consecutive Gold Gloves.

1964: Flood makes the All Star team for the first time in his career; the Cardinals win the World Series, defeating the New York Yankees in seven games; Flood and his family encounter racial tensions upon moving into a house in Alamo, California; Flood and Collins divorce.

1966: Flood goes the entire season without committing an error; Marvin Miller becomes the first executive director of the Players Association; John Jorgensen is murdered and Johnny Keane dies from a heart attack.

1967: Flood sets the record for consecutive games without an error for an outfielder; Muhammad Ali refuses to serve in the military and is stripped of his heavyweight title; The Cardinals beat the Red Sox in seven games to win the World Series.

1968: Martin Luther King and Robert Kennedy are assassinated; track athletes Tommie Smith and John Carlos stage a Black Power protest at the summer Olympics; the Cardinals lose the World Series to the Detroit Tigers in seven games.

1969: On October 8, Flood, Tim McCarver, Joe Hoerner, and Byron Browne are traded to the Philadelphia Phillies for Dick Allen, Cookie Rojas and Jerry Johnson; Flood announces his retirement; in early December, representatives from the Players Association agree to financially support Flood's suit against Major League Baseball.

1970: In January, Flood publicly announces his intention to sue Major League Baseball, contending that the reserve system is a violation of antitrust laws as well as the Thirteenth Amendment; Flood's trial is held from May 19 through June 10 in Federal District Court in Manhattan; Flood moves to Denmark; Judge Irving Ben Cooper rules against Flood, upholding Baseball's antitrust exemption; Flood returns to the States in November and signs a one-year, $110,000 contract to play for the Washington Senators in 1971.

1971: Flood's case is defeated by the Court of Appeals in March; Flood leaves the Senators and relocates to Spain in April.

1972: The Supreme Court hears Flood's case in March; the Players Association goes on strike for 13 days in April; in June, the Supreme Court upholds Baseball's antitrust exemption, 5-3.

1975: In December, arbitrator Peter Seitz awards free agency to pitchers Andy Messersmith and Dave McNally, marking the end of the reserve system.

1978: Flood gets a job as a color analyst on the radio covering the Oakland A's' games.

1988: Flood becomes commissioner of The Senior League.

1994: Flood appears in Ken Burns' "Baseball" documentary for PBS.

1997: Flood dies of throat cancer.

GLOSSARY OF TERMS

Barnstorming: The practice by professional baseball teams of traveling around the countryside to play exhibition games, most often against local ball clubs but sometimes against another traveling squad. Largely extinct today, barnstorming was a common activity of major league teams in decades past as a way of making money and increasing their fan base.

Basic Agreement: The result of collective bargaining (see *Collective Bargaining*) in baseball, it constitutes the governing terms of the relationship between all players and teams, including limitations on the contracts that individual players sign with individual teams.

Bonus Baby: A touted young prospect who received a large signing bonus upon turning professional. The classic bonus baby era began in the late 1940s and continued through 1965. During this time, major league rules specified that an amateur player receiving a bonus above a certain sum could not be farmed out but instead had to remain on the active big league roster for a minimum period (a proviso intended to curb rash spending by the wealthier clubs). The era ended when baseball adopted the amateur free agent draft, which limited the negotiations for each prospect to a single team.

Collective Bargaining: A system of bargaining in which chosen representatives of union employees negotiate with representatives of employers to determine conditions of employment, like wages, rules, and working conditions.

Expansion Era: A common term for the period from 1961 to 1969. Baseball's first expansion in the modern era took place in 1961, when the Los Angeles Angels and the new Washington Senators joined the American League. Three further expansions occurred in 1962 and 1969, increasing the number of major league baseball teams from sixteen in 1960 to twenty-four by 1969. Three subsequent expansions in 1977, 1993, and 1998 have increased the total to thirty.

Farm System: In a farm system, major league teams own or have working relationships with minor league teams. Players can be promoted from and demoted to the farm system at the major league team's discretion. Every major league franchise now has a farm system, and only a few minor leagues operate independently of Major League Baseball. Branch Rickey is credited with developing the first modern farm system in the 1920s.

Federal Baseball: A 1922 Supreme Court case that ruled that antitrust laws did not apply to baseball because it was not deemed interstate commerce.

Free Agent: A player who has no obligation to play for any team and is free to sell his services to any club.

Hot Stove League: The popular term for baseball talk, mostly concerning trades and signings, during the off-season.

Grievance Arbitration: A process in which two parties submit a disagreement regarding something in the collective bargaining agreement to an impartial arbitrator (see *Impartial Arbitrator*), who is appointed by both sides. This method was instituted in the 1968 Basic Agreement.

Impartial Arbitrator: A neutral individual chosen to settle disputes between two parties. While the commissioner was originally tabbed as the arbiter of disagreements between management and the players, the 1970 basic agreement (see *Basic Agreement*) called for an independent arbitrator to rule on all disputes other than those that affected "the integrity of the game."

Jim Crow laws: A legal system of American apartheid that enforced the systematic segregation of and discrimination against African Americans. It was especially prevalent in the South from the end of Reconstruction through the 1960s. More than a racial caste system, it was a way of life.

Negro Leagues: From the Depression until the color barrier was broken by Jackie Robinson in 1947, the Negro National League (founded in 1933) and Negro American League (founded in 1937) showcased some of the country's greatest baseball talent. The Negro National League disbanded shortly after the major leagues integrated. The Negro American League did not close its doors for good until 1962, though the level of play was not nearly so good after integration as it was during its heyday in the 1930s and 1940s.

Option Clause: see *Reserve Clause*

Pacific Coast League: One of the premier high-level minor leagues in the first half of the twentieth century, the Pacific Coast League made a strong push to become recognized as a third major league in the late 1940s and early 1950s. However, with the move of the Brooklyn Dodgers to Los Angeles and the New York Giants to San Francisco in 1958, it quickly became just another minor league, whose teams, previously independent, were all part of major league farm systems (see *Farm Systems*). The Hollywood Stars, Los Angeles Angels, Oakland Oaks, Portland Beavers, Sacramento Solons, San Diego Padres, San Francisco Seals, and Seattle Rainiers were the teams comprising the PCL in its most successful years.

Reserve Clause: A series of provisions of the standard player's contract, which bound a player to one team in perpetuity. Paragraph 10a, the crux of these provisions, provided that the team could renew a contract for an additional year after the contract had expired.

Reserve System: The system created by the owners' use of the reserve clause, in which players could not become free agents but had to play for their teams until they were traded or released.

Salary Arbitration: The process of negotiating salary through an impartial arbitrator. Baseball adopted salary arbitration in 1973. The process involved a player and management each submitting a figure, and the arbitrator choosing between the two. In baseball, the arbitrator must choose between the proposals with no middle ground.

Sherman Antitrust Act: A law passed by Congress in 1890 forbidding businesses from combining or conspiring to harm other businesses, or restrain trade. Named after Senator John Sherman from Ohio, it was the first action taken by the federal government to place limitations on big business.

BIBLIOGRAPHY

Anderson, Dave. *Pennant Races*. New York: Doubleday, 1994.

Cepeda, Orlando, and Herb Fagen. *Baby Bull: From Hardball to Hard Time and Back*. Dallas: Taylor, 1998.

Craft, David, and Tom Owens. *Redbirds Revisted: Great Memories and Stories from St. Louis Cardinals*. Chicago: Bonus Books, 1990.

Dewey, and Nicholas Acocella. *The Ball Clubs*. New York: Harper Perennial, 1993.

Fetter, Henry D. *Taking on the Yankees*. New York: W.W. Norton, 2003.

Flood, Curt, with Richard Carter. *The Way It Is*. New York: Trident Press, 1970.

Halberstam, David. *October 1964*. New York: Villard, 1994.

Heylar, John. *Lords of the Realm, the Real History of Baseball*. New York: Villard, 1994

Heiman, Lee, Dave Weiner and Bill Gutman. *When the Cheering Stops*. New York: Macmillan, 1990.

Gibson, Bob, with Lonnie Wheeler. *Stranger to the Game: The Autobiography of Bob Gibson*. New York: Penguin, 1994.

James, Bill. *The Bill James Historical Baseball Abstract*. New York: Villard Books, 1988.

Kiner, Ralph, with Danny Peary. *Baseball Forever*. Triumph: Chicago, 2004.

Koppett, Leonard. *The New Thinking Fan's Guide to Baseball*. New York: Simon and Schuster, 1991.

Korr, Chuck. The End of Baseball As We Knew It: The Players Union, 1960-81. Urbana and Chicago: University of Illinois Press, 2002.

Kuhn, Bowie. *Hardball: The Education of a Baseball Commissioner.* New York: Times Books, 1987.

Lewis, Anthony. *Gideon's Trumpet.* New York: Random House, 1964.

McCarver, Tim, with Ray Robinson. *Oh, Baby I Love It!* New York: Dell Books, 1987.

Miller, Marvin. *A Whole Different Ballgame: The Inside Story of Baseball's New Deal.* New York: Simon and Schuster, 1991.

Moffi, Larry and Jonathan Kronstadt. *Crossing the Line: Black Major Leagues, 1947-1959.* Iowa City: University of Iowa Press, 1994

Neyer, Rob. *Rob Neyer's Big Book of Baseball Lineups.* New York: Simon and Schuster, 2003.

Peary, Danny. *We Played the Game: 65 Players Remember Baseball's Greatest Era.* New York: Hyperion, 1994.

Raines, Rob. *The St. Louis Cardinals, the 100th Anniversary.* New York: St. Martin's Press, 1992.

Robinson, Frank and Berry Stainback. *Extra Innings.* New York: McGraw-Hill, 1988.

Robinson, Ray. *Stan Musial: Baseball's Durable Man.* New York: G.P. Putnam's Sons, 1963.

Sumner, Jim L. *Separating the Mend From the Boys: The First Half-Century of the Caroline League.* Winston-Salem: North Carolina, 1994.

Tygiel, Jules. *Baseball's Great Experiment: Jackie Robinson and His Legacy.* New York: Oxford University Press, 1983.

Ward, Geoffrey C, and Ken Burns. *Baseball: An Illustrated History.* New York: Alfred A. Knopf, 1994.

Whitfield, Shelby. *Kiss it Goodbye.* New York: Abelard-Schuman, 1973.

Whitford, David. *Extra Innings: A Season in the Senior League.* New York: Harper Collins, 1991.

Woodward, Bob, and Scott Armstrong. *The Brethren: Inside the Supreme Court.* New York: Simon and Schuster, 1979.

ACKNOWLEDGMENTS

I first learned about Curt Flood's story when I worked as a post-production intern on Ken Burns's 1994 PBS documentary about the history of baseball. Sitting in a corner of a dark mixing studio in New York, I saw Flood's face, weathered yet delicate, his eyes glassy. His interviews for the series made an immediate and lasting impression. Flood did not seem like your ordinary ballplayer. I am only sorry that I didn't act sooner to learn more about his life first-hand; he passed away three years after *Baseball* originally aired.

Nine years later, I was approached to write a book about an athlete. Who could be a more fitting subject than Flood, whose autobiography, long out-of-print, was the only major work devoted to his life? *Stepping Up* could not have been written without the generosity and assistance of a number of people. I'd like to take a moment here to recognize them.

First and foremost, I want to thank my editor, Gabe Fried, who has shown great care and patience with me, and whose skills as an editor have made me a better, more conscious writer. He's first class all the way, and I am fortunate to be able to call him as a friend as well.

I would also like to express my gratitude to others at or associated with Persea Books who have supported *Stepping Up*: Karen Braziller, Michael Braziller, Lytton Smith, Rita Lascaro, Laura Ogar, Enid Stubin, and Leslie Goldman.

I did a lot of research for this project, looking through old newspaper clippings as well as articles from *The Sporting News*, *Sport* magazine, and *Sports Illustrated*. Without the invaluable support of Linda Levine of the *Sports Illustrated* library and Steve Lavoie of the Oakland History Room, this book simply would not have been possible. I am deeply in their debt. Larry Abraham at the Fordham Law Library was good enough to explain the legalities of Flood's case to me once, twice, until it finally sunk in. Dave Smith at Retrosheet provided me with box scores and game summaries from every game Flood played in. Rich at the National Archives and Gail Malmgreen at the New York University Law Library, where Marvin Miller's papers are located, were accommodating as well.

Allen Zerman, Max Gitter, and Dan Levitt all shared their memories of Flood and his case. Dan was particularly helpful with my numerous follow-up questions. I can't thank Jay Topkis enough for taking the time on several occasions to speak with me and to look at some early drafts of this book. Jay is a true gentleman and was kind enough to teach me a lesson about handing someone careless work to read without being condescending or cruel in the process. The lesson was well learned.

There are portions of Flood's life that remain a mystery to me, as it was difficult to gain access to certain of his friends and members of his family. However, I am greatly indebted to those friends and family members who did speak to me, particularly his daughter Debbie Flood. Flood's friends and colleagues—including Earl Robinson, Martin Wyatt, Sam Bercovich, Buddy Gilbert, Donn Johnson, Joe Camacho, Dick Groat, Orlando Cepeda, Tim McCarver, Marvin Miller, Mike Morgan, Bing Devine, Jim Bouton, Buck O'Neil, and Harry Edwards—were enormously helpful in giving me a better idea of what he was like. Gene Orza and Steve Rogers at the Players Association were both very obliging, too.

I also want to thank the writers and historians who gave me a deeper understanding of both baseball and social history; including Roger Angell, Taylor Branch, Bill James, Rob Neyer, David Halberstam, George Will, Allen Barra, Ken Burns, Tom Verducci, Buster Olney, Bruce Markusen, Bill Weiss, the late Doug Pappas, Glenn Stout, Ralph Wimpish, Jane Leavy, Gerald Early, Jules Tygiel, Richard Lapchick,

Maury Brown, and the good people at SABR. Chuck Korr was especially giving with his time, thoughts, and connections, for which I am grateful.

I am deeply regretful that I did not have the opportunity to talk to Leonard Koppett, who covered the Flood trial for both the *New York Times* and *The Sporting News* in the concise and balanced manner that distinguished him as one of the great sportswriters of all time. Koppett passed away shortly before I began my research. I hope in some small way he would have approved of my efforts. He is very much a role model.

Walter Dean Myers and Pat Jordan, two writers I have a great deal of respect for, gave me some terrific writing tips. My good pals Alex Ciepley and Rich Lederer were supportive throughout, giving me notes on my writing and answering my endless stream of questions. They are wonderful friends and I'm glad they are on my team. Steve Treder was also instrumental in shaping the text, making sure that I got my facts straight. I also received encouragement and assistance from Brian Gunn, Steven Goldman, Jay Jaffe, Will Carroll, Cliff Corcoran, Jon Weisman, Tim Marchman, Hank Waddles, Neil deMause, Dayn Perry, Ed Cossette, David Pinto, Jacob Luft, Steve Stein, Chris Kahrl, and Greg Spira. And of course, I got lots of moral support from my mom and dad, Kathy and Tom, my sister Sam, Dee and Charlie Shapiro, Frank Nigro, Liz Plummer, E-Double, Greg G, Joey La P, Mike C, Big Jav, Studes, Repoz, Bis and Frek, Jonah and Jenn, Jared, Chris DeRosa, Tracy Bennett, Robert Zieger, Alan Friedman, John Parthum, Shannon Plumb, Paula, Steven Winslow, Steven Cope (my main man), and all of my pals at BaseballToaster.com. Of course, I can't forget to mention my brother Ben, my oldest and greatest teammate.

Last, but certainly not least, I want to say how fortunate I've been to receive the love and support of my girlfriend

Emily Shapiro, who has truly been my biggest fan from the moment I started writing this book. She's a true gem, and she even likes baseball too! How lucky can a guy get? She inspired me to follow my dream and encouraged me every step of the way. Shappie, you are a true angel.

I am blessed to have such loving people in my life, and I want to let them know—even if I forgot to mention them all by name—how much I appreciate them and value their friendship.

INDEX